US Department of the Space Force:

A Necessary Evolution

Dr. John D. Cinnamon, Ph.D.

ABSTRACT

In 2008, the Independent Assessment Panel on the Organization and Management of National Security Space (NSS) reported to Congress that the military and intelligence space programs are fragmented, disorganized, inefficient, and ineffective. Without strong leadership and a unifying vision, the United State (US) space enterprise is losing its advantage over competing nations. The nation must address this erosion of capability with vigor in the near term. Inaction threatens US national interests. The US should create a separate military Department of the Space Force.

This work begins with a summary of the current strategic space environment, examines the fragmented state of the existing space enterprise, and establishes a framework for evaluating NSS. Having established the current NSS environment, it examines the genesis of the US Air Force (USAF). Air and airpower possess a set of specific characteristics that justify a distinct military service. This work then evaluates space and spacepower using the same series of attributes that validate a separate Air Force. Based on these attributes, the unique characteristics of space and space forces require the creation of a new Space Force. This work offers an organizational evolution for the current US space enterprise to address the significant issues that threaten the nation's ability to achieve national objectives. This necessary evolution is a Department of the Space Force.

DEDICATION

Fear not, I am with you; be not dismayed;

I am your God.

I will strengthen you, and help you,

and uphold you with my right hand.

Isaiah 41:10

To my wife

& children:

Thank you for

your love

&

support.

TABLE OF CONTENTS

Contents

A separate space force would benefit the taxpayer, it would benefit the military, and it would benefit the Air Force.

General Charles A. "Chuck" Horner[1]

INTRODUCTION

"Today, no one's in charge." Using these words, the Independent Assessment Panel on the Organization and Management of National Security Space (NSS) reported to Congress that the military and intelligence space programs are fragmented, disorganized, inefficient, and ineffective.[2] Without strong leadership and a unifying vision, the United State (US) space enterprise is losing its advantage over competing nations. The nation must address this erosion of capability with vigor in the near term. Inaction threatens US national interests.[3]

This introduction provides a summary of the current strategic space environment, examines the fragmented state of the existing space enterprise, and establishes a framework for the remainder of the work. Having established the current space enterprise environment, Chapter 1 examines the historical creation of the US Air Force (USAF). The genesis of the USAF provides a set of specific characteristics that formed the foundation of the new service. Chapters 2 through 5 then evaluate the current space forces using the same series of attributes that justified the creation of a separate Air Force. In terms of these attributes, this paper focuses on how the unique characteristics of space and space forces require the creation of a new Space Force. Chapter 6 offers an

---

[1] Steven Watkins, "Defense Trends: Is the space mission too big to handle?" *Air Force Times*, October 7, 1996, 32.

[2] Institute for Defense Analysis, *Leadership, Management, and Organization for National Security Space: Report to Congress of the Independent Assessment Panel on the Organization and Management of National Security Space*, by A. Thomas Young, et al., Office of the Under Secretary of Defense for Policy, (Washington D.C., July 2008), i.

[3] Ibid., ES-6.

organizational evolution to address the significant issues, which threaten the nation's ability to achieve national objectives, in the current US space enterprise. This work proposes that the US should create a separate military Department of the Space Force.

Current Strategic Space Environment

The President of the United States wrote in the 2010 National Space Policy that the "... United States considers the sustainability, stability, and free access to, and use of, space vital to its national interests."[4] Similarly, the 2012 national strategic guidance documents highlight the use of space as a critical element of national power. However, significant emerging threats jeopardize the national ability to exploit space.

Strategic guidance supports the concept that space utilization is crucial to national interests. The 2010 National Security Strategy highlights the vulnerability of the space segment of national power and emphasizes the requirement for the nation to protect space access.[5] This national strategy description acknowledges that adversaries would seek to deny open utilization of the space domain. The 2010 Quadrennial Defense Review stresses the importance of the space architecture and its contribution to US national defense.[6] This comprehensive review also describes the importance of space assets to the entire joint military enterprise and the need to improve the nation's ability to ensure access to space.[7] In addition, the 2011 National Military Strategy recognizes the critical nature of space capability, but characterizes space as a strategic environment that is

---

[4] U.S. President, *National Space Policy* (Washington DC: Government Printing Office, June 28, 2010), 3.

[5] U.S. President, *National Security Strategy* (Washington DC: Government Printing Office, May 2010), 8, 49.

[6] U.S. Department of Defense, *Quadrennial Defense Review Report* (Washington DC: Government Printing Office, February 2010), 33.

[7] Ibid., v-ix.

"congested, contested, and competitive."[8] The 2011 National Security Space Strategy

reaches the same conclusion, along with a description of the emerging danger of other

nations and non-state actors developing competing space and counterspace capabilities.[9]

The recently published 2012 Presidential strategic guidance extends the

proposition that space is a contested domain in which the US must improve its

capabilities to protect the critically important space infrastructure.[10] The 2012

companion budget document, which outlines US military spending choices within a

constrained fiscal environment, specifically protects space capabilities.[11] Consequently,

the ability to access and operate effectively in space is a primary mission of the US armed

forces. This new strategic guidance also directs implementation of the newly authored

2012 Joint Operational Access Concept (JOAC). The JOAC emphasizes a contested

space and cyberspace environment as one of three major trends negatively affecting US

capability to access critical domains and project national power. [12] Specifically,

adversaries will target space assets as part of their anti-access campaigns and ". . .

arguably, this emergence is the most important and fundamental change in the opposed

access challenge over the past several decades."[13]

Essentially, the US strategic guidance documents weave a common theme of

national strategic dependence on space capability. However, these works also allude to

---

[8] Chairman of the Joint Chiefs of Staff, *The National Military Strategy of the United States of America* (Washington DC: Government Printing Office, 2011), 3.

[9] U.S. Secretary of Defense and U.S. Director of National Intelligence, *National Security Space Strategy* (Washington DC: Government Printing Office, January 2011), 1.

[10] U.S. Department of Defense, *Sustaining U.S. Global Leadership: Priorities for the 21st Century Defense* (Washington DC: Government Printing Office, January 2012), 3-5.

[11] U.S. Department of Defense, *Defense Budget Priorities and Choices* (Washington DC: Government Printing Office, January 2012), 10.

[12] U.S. Department of Defense, *Joint Operational Access Concept (JOAC)* (Washington DC: Government Printing Office, 17 January 2012), Forward.

[13] Ibid., 6, 12.

threats to the national interests through the space domain and a growing need to act to preserve space capability. Acknowledging the strategic importance of space to the national interests requires an examination of the effectiveness of the US national space enterprise.

Current Status of the National Security Space Enterprise

The Independent Assessment Panel on the Organization and Management of National Security Space (NSS), commonly referred to as the Allard Commission, expressed grave concern over the condition of NSS and noted that it requires the highest level of urgency.[14] The scope of the commission's report was the entire NSS, comprising all military, intelligence, other government agency, and commercial space assets and capabilities. The Allard Commission concluded that US leadership in space was an absolutely essential national advantage.[15] However, due to fragmented leadership, the NSS effectiveness is eroding. NSS is experiencing decreasing performance, decreasing capacity, increasing capability gaps and vulnerabilities.[16] In short, the US is ceding the NSS advantage by failing to act to repair this critical national asset and therefore national interests are in jeopardy.[17] The Allard Commission report highlights four areas of critical concern with regard to the current state of NSS.

The first struggling area of NSS is space systems acquisition. This effort is fraught with failures, delays, and cost overruns. As a generalization of the NSS programs, acquisition efforts have resulted in systems that are twice the original cost

---

[14] Institute for Defense Analysis, *Leadership, Management, and Organization*, July 2008, ES-6.
[15] Ibid., ES-2.
[16] Ibid.
[17] Ibid., ES-3.

and average six years late.[18] The amount of money in these overruns is significant. For

instance, as illustrated in Figure 1, from fiscal years (FY) 1996 to 2008, cost overruns

reported in 2009 amount to approximately $18 billion (in FY 2009 dollars) for seven

unclassified space programs.[19] For FY 2008 to FY 2013, the costs are $10.9 billion more

than initial estimates (in FY 2009 dollars).[20] These cost overruns keep increasing. For

instance, the same seven unclassified programs had reported an estimated $14 billion cost

overrun in 2008 – a $4 billion difference in just one year.[21] In addition, many of the

Total Cost Differences from Program Start to Most Recent Estimates

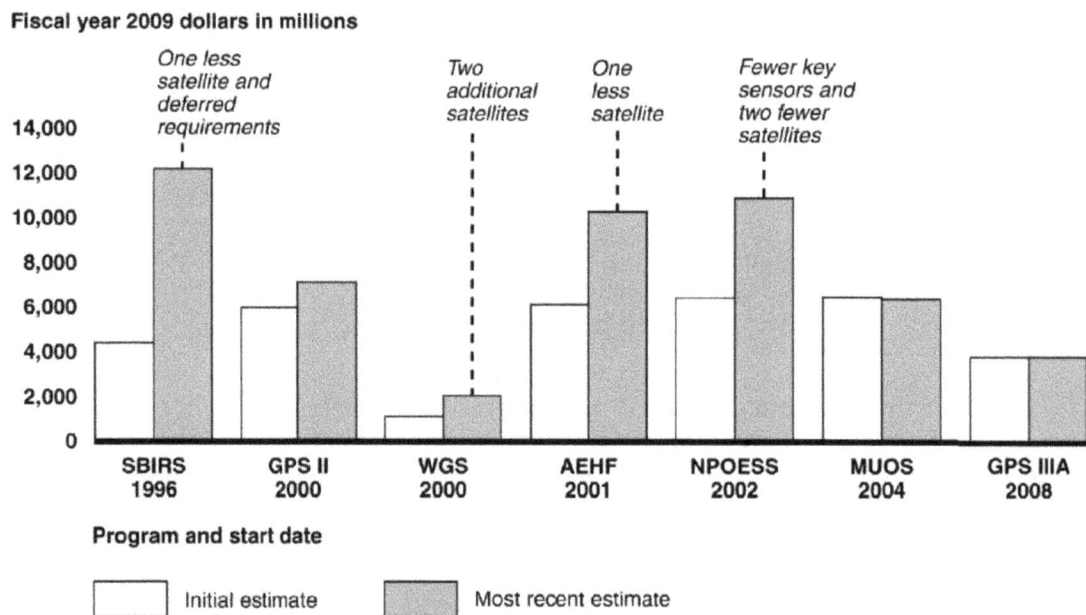

Fiscal year 2009 dollars in millions

Source: GAO analysis of DOD data.

Legend: SBIRS = Space Based Infrared System, GPS = Global Positioning System, WGS = Wideband Global SATCOM, AEHF = Advanced Extremely High Frequency, NPOESS = National Polar-orbiting Operational Environmental Satellite System, and MUOS = Mobile User Objective System.

Figure 1. Cost Overruns in the NSS Enterprise, FY1996-2008 [20]

---

[18] Institute for Defense Analysis, *Leadership, Management, and Organization*, July 2008, 4.

[19] Government Accountability Office, *Space Acquisitions: DOD Faces Substantial Challenges in Developing New Space Systems,* GAO-09-705T (Washington D.C., 20 May 2009), i.

[20] Ibid., i.

[21] Government Accountability Office, *Space Acquisitions: Major Space Programs Still at Risk for Cost and Schedule Increases,* GAO-08-552T (Washington D.C., 4 May 2008), 3.

systems are years late and underperform acquisition requirements. These NSS failures create almost $2 billion per year in cost overruns and immeasurable losses in national space capability and power projection opportunities – and these are only the unclassified space programs. Similar issues plague classified space systems. According to the Allard Commission, these NSS shortcomings (including classified and unclassified efforts) are attributable to a lack of sufficient technical personnel, fragmented programs across the government, and weak management.[22] Pockets of excellence exist, and space personnel are working diligently to improve the NSS enterprise.[23] The system itself, however, hinders their efforts and makes success impossible.

The second area of concern is that the historical separation of military and intelligence space efforts only serves to guarantee continued failures to fix the acquisition and operational NSS issues.[24] In general, military space programs are unclassified and the intelligence community (IC) programs, led by the National Reconnaissance Office (NRO), are classified. During the Cold War, the separation of these communities was justified.[25] However, since the beginning of this century, the NRO has ". . . not provide[d] a single capability that fulfilled its full potential. It either failed, was shot down or shut down" according to Allard Commission panel member, General Edward Anderson.[26] The disparate cultures in the military and IC space communities have led to disagreements on acquisition and operational issues that simply prohibit mission

---

[22] Institute for Defense Analysis, *Leadership, Management, and Organization*, July 2008, 4-5.
[23] Ibid., 5.
[24] Ibid., 5-8.
[25] Ibid., 6.
[26] Sharon L. Hartman, "An Inside Look at the Allard Commission… And That's the Way it Was," *Army Space Journal* (Summer 2009), 24.

accomplishment.[27] The Commission concluded that the NSS enterprise must merge under a single architecture to avoid "guarantee[d] failure" in achieving necessary program improvements.[28]

The third area requiring immediate attention is that space technology is proliferating to other nations and non-state actors, thereby threatening space assets. The Allard Commission concluded that there are rapidly emerging foreign space capabilities that are outside the US span of control.[29] This proliferation of space technology challenges US preeminence and undermines international standing.[30] Additionally, outdated International Traffic in Arms Regulation export regulations restrict the competitive potential of the NSS enterprise industry and damage US national space capability.[31] Ironically, some efforts to prevent space technology export have driven other technology leaders to sell their space expertise to adversaries. This proliferation of space technology has allowed adversary actors to gain the capacity to challenge US space access and damage space assets.[32] The fragmented state of NSS, in terms of leadership and responsibility to protect the space infrastructure, prohibits the US from formulating a coherent response to these threats.[33] The US needs to respond immediately to counter space technology proliferation and confront adversary efforts to deny space access in order to preserve national capabilities.

---

[27] Joan Johnson-Freese, "An Allard Commission Postmortem and the Need for a National Space Council," *Joint Forces Quarterly* 60,1 (Winter 2011), 55.

[28] Institute for Defense Analysis, *Leadership, Management, and Organization*, July 2008, 8.

[29] Ibid., 8.

[30] Center for Strategic & International Studies (CSIS), *Briefing of the Working Group on the Health of the U.S. Space Industrial Base and the Impact of Export Controls* (Washington DC: CSIS, February 2008), 20-22.

[31] Institute for Defense Analysis, *Leadership, Management, and Organization*, July 2008, 8-9.

[32] Ibid., 9-10.

[33] Ibid.

Finally, the Allard report highlighted organizational changes in NSS that weakened leadership in this critical arena. Essentially, NSS has fragmented in recent years to such a degree that leadership and management is impossible.[34] Figure 2 (see list of abbreviations at the end of this work) is an illustration of the current organizational structure of NSS.[35] This creates a convoluted NSS structure with no clear lines of authority or leadership. A number of government agencies are managing, as opposed to leading, NSS by a partially achieved and mostly ineffective consensus. Allard Commission Chairman, A. Thomas Young, concluded, ". . . there has been 'no adult supervision' in national security space."[36] This dysfunctional leadership is not the result

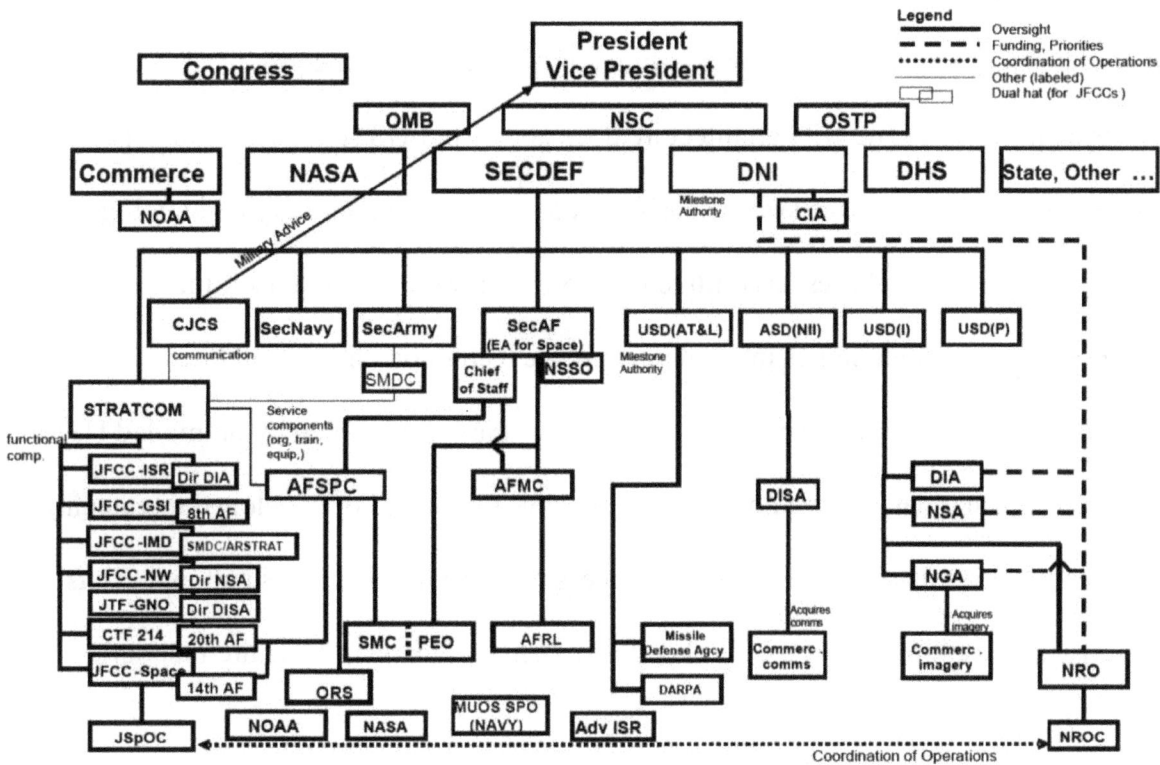

Figure 2. Current Organization of the NSS [35]

---

[34] Institute for Defense Analysis, *Leadership, Management, and Organization*, July 2008, 11-14.
[35] Ibid., 14.
[36] Amy Butler, "Adrift in Space," *Aviation Week & Space Technology* 169,14 (13 October 2008), 34.

of a lack of effort. The Air Force is the Executive Agent for Space, and ". . . has done nothing short of a spectacular job of bringing the US to its current pre-eminence in space."[37] However, the Air Force has suffered from an eroding authority over the NSS architecture and a diffuse structure that stymies leadership. The Allard Commission concluded that NSS is in dire need of top-to-bottom reorganization in order to secure US national objectives.[38] The Committee on US Space Leadership determined ". . . there are serious, systemic problems which portend a broad erosion of US leadership and advantage in space. The United States is at a seminal point in the evolution of space as a vital national enterprise."[39]

The current state of the NSS enterprise is dire. The space acquisition community in NSS has failed to deliver systems on-time, on-budget, and at the promised performance levels. The NSS architecture does not permit US space professionals to succeed in developing space systems. The disconnect between military and intelligence space structures and cultures has outlived any previous rationale and usefulness. In order to succeed, these communities must merge. Space technology has proliferated to economic competitors and to political adversaries. Partially enabled by outmoded US export laws, other nations and non-state actors have purchased or developed threatening space capabilities that could deny the US access to space or damage its national assets. Underlying the entire NSS is a convoluted and diffuse leadership structure that defies

---

[37] James B. Armor, Jr., "The Air Force's Other Blind Spot," *The Space Review* (15 September 2008), 3.

[38] Institute for Defense Analysis, *Leadership, Management, and Organization*, July 2008, ES-4.

[39] Committee on U.S. Space Leadership, "Memorandum for the President: America's Leadership in Space," *Space Policy* (10 March 2009), 3.

understanding and fails to function appropriately. Leadership of NSS could repair the enterprise and enable space assets to support US national objectives effectively.

A Framework for Evaluating the Way Forward

One way to examine this need for a complete reorganization of the NSS enterprise is within the historical context. A similar effort to streamline the leadership of a unique national capability occurred after World War II with regard to the nation's air forces. The US government created a separate Department of the Air Force immediately following the successful conclusion of World War II. The US Army Air Force's decisive contributions to the Allied victories formed the backdrop for this national debate. National leaders recognized that airpower possessed some unique qualities and capabilities that required the creation of a new military service to exploit. Chapter 1 examines this historical example in greater detail. Four primary characteristics of airpower led the nation to create a separate military department: air is a unique medium; airpower is an evolution in technology; airpower development requires distinct leadership, doctrine, and funding; and airpower delivers strategic impacts and is vitally important to the nation. This example provides a framework to evaluate the unique characteristics of space forces.

Chapters 2 through 5 highlight the various unique aspects of the NSS enterprise along the same lines developed in Chapter 1. These chapters examine the characteristics of NSS, parallel to those in Chapter 1, which justified the creation of a separate Air Force. This work also describes the primary competing notion that the current "aerospace" system can exploit these attributes. Each presentation develops both the view that these elements justify a separate service and the argument that space forces need to remain within the existing structure.

Finally, Chapter 6 proposes an organizational structure that answers the challenge of the Allard Commission and promises to secure national interests more efficiently and effectively. This new service will unify space efforts and ensure these assets make a greater contribution to the national strategic ends. A United States Space Force could save the nation billions of dollars by leading NSS with a clear, understandable, and fiscally efficient architecture. General Chuck Horner concluded, in the quote that leads this introduction, a separate space force would save the American taxpayer money, would improve military capability, and would benefit the US Air Force. This new military department offers a bold solution to the issues outlined by the Allard Commission.

Summary

Currently, NSS is disorganized and inefficient. History, in the genesis of the US Air Force, offers an example of how to create order and effectiveness out of a unique capability. The rationale for creating the Air Force in 1947 parallels the status of US space forces in 2012. Indeed, tracing the same logic used by the national leadership in the 1940s, a separate Space Force service is necessary to capitalize on the unique nature of space. The nation can devise a new Space Force from the elements of existing organizations that will address the Allard Commission's criticisms and secure national interests in the high frontier. The United States should create a separate military Department of the Space Force.

. . . the Air Commander and his staff are an organization coordinate with and coequal to the land forces and the Navy. I realize there can be other individual opinions. . . But that seems to be so logical from all of our experiences in this war—such an inescapable conclusion—that I for one can't entertain any longer any doubt as to its wisdom.

General Dwight D. Eisenhower[1]

CHAPTER 1: CREATING THE DEPARTMENT OF THE US AIR FORCE

In 1947, the United States (US) government created a separate US Air Force (USAF) as a distinct military department. A significant political process,[2] with passionate arguments on both sides of the issue, was required for this immense change in the military organization.[3] The nation created this new service, focused on the domination and exploitation of air, prompted partially by airpower's pivotal contribution to Allied victory in World War II (WWII). Adding to this impetus was the acknowledgment that air possessed some very distinct characteristics and challenges. US national leadership recognized that airpower required its own military service because air was a substantially different medium from the surface domains. In addition, airpower represented a significant evolution in technology. In order to ensure air domination, Airmen required their own leadership, doctrine, and funding source distinct from land forces. Finally, effective airpower use delivered unique strategic effects and demonstrated its importance to the nation.

---

[1] Charles M. Westenhoff, "Why we Need an Air Force,"*Joint Force Quarterly* (Autumn/Winter 1994-95), 65.
[2] Charles A. Stevenson, "The Story Behind the National Security Act of 1947," *Military Review* 88, 3 (May/June 2008), 13.
[3] C. V. Glines, "The Long Road to an Independent Air Force," *Aviation Story* 18, 1 (Sep 2007), 30.

Air Force Performance in World War II

The semi-autonomous US Army Air Forces (USAAF) performed exceptionally well during WWII. This success became one of the driving forces in the process to create a separate USAF. Airpower proved itself to be a powerful military capability as it had delivered significant combat effects against the enemy forces. Airpower was a critical element that ensured the victory of Allied forces.

During WWII, the Allies used airpower in a variety of ways. In some cases, they employed airpower to defeat enemy air forces; ensuring Allied ground forces were safe from enemy air attack. In other applications, airpower was used directly against enemy ground forces while they were in contact with the Allied troops. Ground commanders realized that without air dominance, the ground battle was drastically more difficult, if not impossible. Field Marshall Rommel concluded in his notes that Allied airpower was the single most important factor in the ground fight and was the key to victory on the ground.[4] General Eisenhower came to the same conclusion during his time commanding Allied forces in WWII. He made the comment that without air supremacy during the Normandy invasion, he would not have been successful.[5] Many land-force commanders, like General Douglas MacArthur, concluded that airpower could create an overwhelming advantage for the ground combat effort.[6]

While Air forces had become indispensable to achieving victory for ground forces, perhaps the most effective use of airpower's potential was realized when it was used against strategic targets behind enemy lines. Airpower demonstrated that it was

---

[4] B. H. Liddell-Hart, ed., *The Rommel Papers* (New York: Da Capo Press, 1953), 328.
[5] Westenhoff, *Joint Force Quarterly*, Autumn/Winter 1994-95, 63.
[6] Ibid., 63.

extraordinarily and uniquely effective in extending Allied reach and power projection deep into enemy territory.[7] Airpower made critical contributions to the war effort in battle after battle across the globe in WWII and proved it could provide dominating combat effects. In some cases, airpower was the single most important factor in achieving the strategic goals.[8] As a result, General Eisenhower became an important advocate for a separate Air Force in the post-war discussion on the organization of the future military. He believed that airpower was the essential key to the victory of ground forces and that the US needed to organize and employ air forces autonomously.[9]

In the post-WWII era, a political debate ensued over the issue of creating a separate Air Force department. The decisive nature of airpower's contributions to the nation's victory in WWII created an impetus for the new service. Advocates of this new military service justified their rationale with the unique characteristics of airpower and its employment.

Air is a Unique Medium

One of the themes that formed the basis for the arguments to separate air forces from the Army was the recognition of air as a distinct medium. Air, as a location in which forces could exist, transit, and employ combat power is fundamentally different from the land and sea.[10] This medium, which could be accessed from anywhere on the globe and allow operations across the planet, was so different that a separate cadre of

---

[7] Robert J. Elder, "Air-Mindedness," *Air & Space Power Journal* 23, 3 (Fall 2009), 13.
[8] Ibid., 13.
[9] Herman S. Wolk, "Ike and the Air Force," *Air Force Magazine* (April 2006), 85-86.
[10] Mark A. Clodfelter, "Molding Airpower Convictions: Development and Legacy of William Mitchell's Strategic Thought," In *The Paths of Heaven: the Evolution of Airpower Theory* (Maxwell Air Force Base: Air University Press, 1997), 101.

personnel was required to capitalize on its potential.[11] This third dimension is fundamentally different from the surface mediums. Airpower theorists (e.g. Billy Mitchell) developed ideas for using air as a distinct location for conflict and combat advantage almost immediately after the Wright brothers flew their first aircraft.[12] The nation now had access to a new medium.

Others claimed that airpower was simply an extension of Army fires – i.e. an airborne delivery system for artillery. However, those that fought in ground engagements in WWII soon realized that the unique nature of air, as a medium, afforded distinctive advantages. Airmen were not blindly flying against set targets, close to the front, and dropping bombs. They were engaged in a fluid environment, conducting strikes on key enemy capabilities with autonomy and initiative. Additionally, exploitation of the air medium required fundamentally different training, mindsets, equipment, and techniques. Perhaps General Carl A. "Tooey" Spaatz summarized the uniqueness of the air medium in the most concise way: "We flew through the air and the other people walked on the ground; it was as simple as that!"[13] Air is therefore a distinct medium, separate from the surface environments, requiring a separate approach and service.[14]

Airpower is an Evolution in Technology

Air domination required an evolution of technology. For centuries prior to the Wright brothers, the human race had attempted, and failed, to achieve flight. Creating

---

[11] James B. Armor, Jr. "Viewpoint: It is Time to Create a United States Air Force Space Corps," *Astropolitics* 5 (2007), 280.

[12] Mark A. Clodfelter, "Molding Airpower Convictions: Development and Legacy of William Mitchell's Strategic Thought," In *The Paths of Heaven: the Evolution of Airpower Theory* (Maxwell Air Force Base: Air University Press, 1997), 82.

[13] Ronald R. Fogleman, "Aerospace Doctrine: More Than Just a Theory," *Airpower Journal* (Summer 1996), 42.

[14] Armor, *Astropolitics*, 2007, 281.

aircraft that could achieve flight required the technology of the internal combustion engine, manufacturing, aerodynamics, advanced materials, and many others. The early air pioneers leveraged these various technological disciplines and created a synergistic product. The aircraft allowed man finally to fly. Flight was an amazing evolutionary accomplishment in the early twentieth century.

Airpower became significant to the US within a few decades. Airpower's application in World War I (WWI) was fairly modest. Aircraft use was largely limited to reconnaissance missions and limited engagement with ground forces close to the war's front lines. Yet, during WWI, aircraft represented an evolution in technology with respect to ground combat systems.[15] From its origins in WWI, airpower's use changed significantly in WWII. Aircraft capability reached levels that allowed both employment deep into enemy territory and persistent support of ground forces. Therefore, airpower's importance on the battlefield increased substantially. Due to this enhanced combat effectiveness, the availability of airpower in the engagements decided the outcome of many battles.[16]

The evolution of technology allowed the development of more capable aircraft. These aircraft continued to improve and gain key characteristics of range, combat load capacity, speed, survivability, and lethality that made airpower a pivotal resource. This technology was so profoundly different from surface technologies that entire industries developed to expand this evolving field. Airpower development relied significantly on continued technological innovation and advancement. This close tie between airpower and technology leads the nation to correctly view airpower as an evolution of technology.

---

[15] Westenhoff, *Joint Force Quarterly*, Autumn/Winter 1994-95, 62-63.
[16] Ibid., 63-64.

Airpower Development Requires Separate Leadership, Doctrine, and Funding

One critical argument for the formation of a separate Air Force was that the

effective use of airpower required distinctive and tailored leadership, specific doctrine,

and separate funding resources. Advocates for a distinct Air Force pointed to a history of

limitations on airpower's contributions to war efforts and a lack of understanding of how

to employ air forces for the maximum combat effect.[17] The arguments for a distinct force

began in WWI and continued until the US established the Air Force in 1947.

One of the primary justifications offered for a separate Air Force was in the area

of leadership. Not surprisingly, airpower enthusiasts were largely in favor of air

leadership separate from surface force commanders.[18] These advocates pointed to the

recent WWII victories that highlighted airpower's decisive nature. Proponents could

clearly link this effectiveness to airpower's employment free of ground commander's

control.[19] In fact, a partial separation between the USAAF and the ground forces was

necessary during WWII. The Army Air Forces maintained its own budget, staffs,

doctrine and promotion lists apart from the rest of the Army.[20] Creating a USAF was the

next obvious step to ensure effective leadership of air forces.

Airpower's success was based both on its autonomy from surface forces and on

its newly formed airpower doctrine.[21] This specific doctrine allowed Airmen to

concentrate forces under central leadership and control, strike critical targets far from the

front lines, and to contribute more effectively to the entire war campaign. Indeed, the

---

[17] Michael C. Whittington, *A Separate Space Force – An 80-Year-Old Argument* (Maxwell Air Force Base: Air University Press, May 2000), 3.

[18] Ibid., 3.

[19] Armor, *Astropolitics*, 2007, 280-281.

[20] Ibid., 280-281.

[21] Ibid.

National Security Act of 1947 charged the Air Force specifically with the responsibility of developing airpower with its associated strategy.[22] General Eisenhower strongly forwarded the argument that the Air Force needed to be a separate entity with its own doctrine and personnel to serve the nation.[23] Air Force specific leadership and doctrine, distinct from the other services, was critical to champion airpower's capabilities and to nurture its contribution to US national interests.

Another motivation for a new military department of the Air Force was funding for aircraft and the associated infrastructure. As the United States began the transition from WWII to a post-war environment, the national leaders were concerned about how to organize the defense establishment to best deter future conflicts. President Truman was convinced that, for optimal strategic planning and appropriations, the defense establishment needed to unify in purpose but organize in three separate services (Army, Navy, and a new Air Force).[24] The nation could guarantee a more effective and efficient defense if the funding for the Air Force could be separated from the parochial concerns of the Army and Navy. Appropriations were constrained in the post-war environment and Congress was specifically interested in limiting the duplication of efforts between the air arm of the Navy and the Air Force. The US could realize budget savings by clearly assigning a bulk of the responsibility for airpower to the Air Force.[25] Creating a new separate service was the only way that airpower could be developed more effectively and efficiently.

---

[22] Westenhoff, *Joint Force Quarterly*, Autumn/Winter 1994-95, 65.

[23] Herman S. Wolk, "Ike and the Air Force," *Air Force Magazine* (April 2006), 87-88.

[24] Herman S. Wolk, *Toward Independence: The Emergence of the U.S. Air Force 1945-1947* (Bolling Air Force Base: Air Force History and Museums Program, 1996), 17.

[25] George H. Monahan, *The Army-Navy Contest for Control of Land-Based Antisubmarine Aviation and the Military Unification Debate, 1942-1948* (Ann Arbor: Proquest, May 2011), 160-161.

Advocates for a new Department of the Air Force argued that Airmen needed to lead airpower and that they are the appropriate authors of air doctrine. Additionally, effective airpower development necessitated a separate budget. With these elements, airpower could achieve its full potential.

Airpower Delivers Strategic Impacts and is Vitally Important to the Nation

Perhaps the most convincing attribute of airpower is that it has inherent strategic impacts if used properly. Closely related to this characteristic is that airpower development and use is vitally important to the nation. Together, these qualities created another impetus to create a separate Air Force.

Airpower, when allowed to, created significant strategic impacts during WWII's battles. Aircraft could, with appropriate defensive systems or armed escort, travel deep behind enemy lines and attack strategic targets.[26] In some cases, airpower alone can defeat enemy armed forces.[27] While debate exists on the extent to which strategic bombing contributed to the Allied victory, it is clear that the strategic nature of air attack on enemy forces, military infrastructure, and national will was unique and significant to the war effort.[28] Additionally, airpower contributed to strategic success by defending Allied ground forces from enemy air attack. Generals MacArthur and Eisenhower both concluded airpower was an essential element for the success of the strategic campaign in WWII.[29] The use of airpower essentially altered the nature of warfare by enabling the projection of combat effects against both strategic targets and the ground campaign.

---

[26] Fogleman, *Airpower Journal*, Summer 1996, 43.

[27] Ibid., 43.

[28] Gian P. Gentile, "A-bombs, budgets, and morality: Using the Strategic Bombing Survey," *Air Power History* 44, 1 (Spring 1997), 23.

[29] Westenhoff, *Joint Force Quarterly*, Autumn/Winter 1994-95, 63-64.

Related to the concept of airpower's unique nature and contribution to the strategic war effort is its importance to the survival and success of the nation. During WWI, the British came to that conclusion and established their separate Air Force as a result of bombing raids against their cities.[30] Many of the US military commanders made the same assessment following WWII. Perhaps the single most effective advocate was General Eisenhower. He argued tirelessly that the Air Force needed to be a separate military department based on airpower's importance to the future of the nation.[31] President Truman also noted airpower's importance, remarking that airpower was equal to land and sea in terms of strategic significance and planning.[32] General Fogleman summarized the vital importance of airpower this way:

> No American soldier has been attacked on the ground by an air-breathing vehicle since 1953. From that experience has grown a general feeling that air superiority is a God-given right of Americans. It just happens. It belongs to us. It's an absolute on the battle field. But nothing could be further from the truth. The reason we have had air superiority over that period of time is the fact that we have a full-service air force that pays attention to these things, that develops the weapon systems, and that moves them forward.[33]

Airpower provides the nation with significant strategic capability and is vitally important to attainment of national objectives. These important facets of airpower contributed to the process of creating a separate Department of the Air Force.

Summary

The US government created the US Air Force in 1947 based on several unique characteristics of airpower and a political drive to ensure airpower's effectiveness in the

---

[30] Westenhoff, *Joint Force Quarterly*, Autumn/Winter 1994-95, 62-63.
[31] Herman S. Wolk, "Ike and the Air Force," *Air Force Magazine* (April 2006), 88.
[32] Ibid., 87.
[33] Fogleman, *Airpower Journal*, Summer 1996, 44.

future. Airpower performed exceptionally well in combat during WWII and was a decisive factor in the Allied victory. Most ground commanders acknowledged that without air supremacy, combat operations became difficult and costly, and sometimes impossible. Airpower possesses four key attributes that proponents enumerated in the effort to justify a separate military department. First, air is a unique medium that offers significant advantages. Second, airpower is an evolutionary step in the technology of warfare and is able to deliver devastating combat effects. Third, for the nation to effectively leverage airpower going forward from WWII, the US needed a new Air Force with its own distinct leadership and personnel, doctrine, and source of funding and appropriations priorities. This new military department would realize budget savings for the nation by locating the preponderance of air assets and air leadership in a single, unified organization. Finally, airpower delivers significant strategic advantages in a war effort and this capability is immensely important to the nation. These factors formed the landscape in which the debates on forming a new military service occurred. Together, they compelled the national leadership in 1947 to support the creation of a new military department. These same factors are useful when the nation once again considers forming a new military department to exploit the unique medium of space with evolving technology. These space forces need their own leadership, doctrine, and funding. This new space force would continue making unparalleled strategic contributions and remain vitally important to the future of the US.

The nation which controls space can control the Earth.
Senator John F. Kennedy, 24 October 1960[1]

CHAPTER 2: SPACE IS A UNIQUE MEDIUM

In 1960, Senator Kennedy highlighted the importance of space exploration and

exploitation to the nation. Even in those early years, the United States (US) recognized

the unique nature of space as an operating environment. Space vehicles can pass over

adversary territory with impunity and provide an unparalleled strategic perspective.

However, this extraordinary capability requires utilizing a medium that is discrete and

unforgiving. The differences between space and other mediums are numerous and

significant. A separate space force is necessary to fully understand and exploit this

distinct environment.

Space is Unique

Space is a unique operating environment. It may share characteristics with

atmospheric operations but it is manifestly distinct. No universal definition of where

exactly space begins currently exists. However, one widely accepted notion is that it

begins where an object can maintain "orbit" around earth -- at approximately 100

kilometers above sea level.[2] (At this minimum orbital altitude, a space vehicle is able to

perform a mission and not decay back into the atmosphere for a substantial period of

time.) This concept of where space begins is critical to space operations because national

---

[1] John F. Kennedy, quoted in William W. Brunner III, "National Security Implications of Inexpensive Space Access," In *Beyond the Paths of Heaven: the Emergence of Space Power Thought* (Maxwell Air Force Base: Air University Press, 1999), 365.
[2] Alexei Arbarov and Vladimir Dvorkin, *Outer Space: Weapons, Diplomacy, and Security* (Washington D.C.: Carnegie Endowment for International Peace, 2010), 3.

claims of sovereignty do not apply to space.[3] Therefore, one must define the boundary between air operations (which may be subject to claims of airspace ownership) and space operations (which are immune from over-flight restrictions).

The space environment is vastly different from the atmosphere.[4] Space is a harsh vacuum with extreme temperatures of heat and cold (depending on sun exposure), radiation, damaging debris, magnetic fields, and weightlessness.[5] To conduct operations in this environment requires special and expensive engineering solutions. Systems put "on orbit" are almost impossible to repair and represent a substantial investment of time and money.[6] Development of vehicles and systems to operate in space requires specialized technologies that are fundamentally different from terrestrial approaches.[7] Examples of these differences include propulsion, communications, life support, thermal control, power generation, and control. In essence, there are far fewer similarities to terrestrial systems than differences. This is because space is a vastly different medium. General Fogleman, former Air Force Chief of Staff, referred to space as the "fourth medium of warfare."[8] The latest US national strategic documents (e.g. 2012 Presidential national strategic guidance,[9] 2012 Joint Operational Access Concept,[10] among others) reflect this concept of space as the fourth medium.

---

[3] Arbarov and Dvorkin, *Outer Space*, 2010, 3.

[4] Gregory Billman, "The Inherent Limitations of Space Power: Fact or Fiction?," In *Beyond the Paths of Heaven: The Emergence of Space Power Thought* (Maxwell Air Force Base: Air University Press, September 1999), 516-522.

[5] Arbarov and Dvorkin, *Outer Space*, 2010, 3.

[6] Ibid., 11.

[7] David N. Spires, *Beyond Horizons: A History of the Air Force in Space, 1947-2007* (Colorado Springs: Air Force Space Command, 2007), 136.

[8] Mark E. Harter, "Ten Propositions Regarding Space Power: The Dawn of a Space Force," *Air & Space Power Journal* 20, 2 (Summer 2006), 67.

[9] U.S. Department of Defense, *Sustaining U.S. Global Leadership: Priorities for the 21st Century Defense* (Washington DC: Government Printing Office, January 2012), 4.

There is a common theme throughout the discussions by those who choose to view air and space as slightly varying manifestations of the same medium. This theme is that of "aerospace." Aerospace is simply everything above the surface of the planet and encompasses air breathing systems and space systems. Some Air Force leaders have called this aerospace a "seamless operational medium."[11] Additionally, while beyond the scope of this paper, some current leaders are expanding this description to include "air, space, and cyberspace."[12] Some similarities do exist between the air and space environments, but to call them seamless or identical is simply erroneous. The fact that some aerospace companies build both aircraft and satellites or that the Air Force is the most significant entity to employ systems in both mediums does not merge them. Similar logic applied to surface forces would require one to view land and sea connected seamlessly at the shoreline.[13] Air Force leaders should be particularly sensitive to the notion that disparate mediums are seamless. Some contemporary authors use this analysis to argue that that Air Force needs to return to the Army because airpower is simply a more complex way to deliver artillery.[14] Fortunately, for the Air Force and US national capability, the national leadership recognizes this viewpoint as parochial and invalid.

Space is dissimilar from the other mediums in key ways. Weapons use in space illustrates the absolute unique nature of space as a medium. In 1962, the US detonated a

---

[10] U.S. Department of Defense, *Joint Operational Access Concept (JOAC)* (Washington DC: Government Printing Office, 17 January 2012), 12.
[11] Ralph Millsap and Posey, D. B., "Organizational Options for the Future Aerospace Force," *Aerospace Power Journal* 14, 2 (Summer 2000), 48.
[12] John A. Shaud and Lowther, Adam B., "An Air Force Strategic Vision for 2020-2030," *Strategic Studies Quarterly* (Spring 2011), 8.
[13] Shawn P. Rife, "On Space-Power Separatism," *Air & Space Power Journal* 13, 1 (Spring 1999), 25.
[14] Robert Farley, "Abolish the Air Force," *The American Prospect* 18, 11 (Nov 2007), 34.

1.4 megaton nuclear device in low-earth orbit. This blast created an electromagnetic pulse that damaged seven satellites, shut down power on the earth in the region, and created orbital effects that rendered that region of space inhospitable for new satellite operations for months.[15] In a similar manner, in 2007 the Chinese conducted anti-satellite operations against one of their aging weather satellites using a kinetic device launched from earth. The result of this clear demonstration of the vulnerability of satellites was an extensive debris field that rendered that specific orbit unusable for decades and now creates a significant hazard to orbits that cross the field for years to come.[16] Actions taken in the space medium are distinct from air operations and have much different consequences. They have longer effects, require highly advanced technologies, and demand a greater degree of understanding and deliberation. Space is therefore a distinctive medium and not an extension of air or part of aerospace.

A Separate Space Force is Needed to Operate In and Capitalize on Space

Space is a distinct and complex medium. To exploit this unique environment, the nation possesses a cadre of space professionals with specialized knowledge, a specific mindset, and space experience. These space force personnel currently work in agencies across the federal government. This space force needs to be independent to utilize space successfully. Advocates of a separate Air Force made similar arguments to split from the Army to focus on employing the air medium. The nation needs a separate space force to realize its full potential in the complex space arena.

---

[15] Michael L. Howard, *Rendezvous in Space – A Look in on Military Space Power* (Carlisle Barracks: U.S. Army War College, 2010), 2.
[16] John E. Shaw, "Guarding the High Ocean," *Air & Space Power Journal* 23, 1 (Spring 2009), 56.

Space is a highly challenging medium to understand and operate within. Space professionals must possess a high degree of expertise in order to ensure success of the expensive systems and complex missions within space.[17] The existing structure of the National Security Space (NSS) enterprise, with specialists and separate career fields within various government agencies, speaks to the veracity of the claim that space professionals are required to exploit this unique environment successfully. Much like the claim by Airmen that only airpower experts truly understand the medium of air, space professionals best understand that medium.[18] When these experts operate within non-space centric organizations and have other duties, their capability suffers.[19] The unique nature of the medium demands a dedicated and separate space force.

Proponents of the aerospace construct contend that being different, however, does not necessarily justify being separate. They propose that in order to claim that the unique medium of space necessitates a new space service demands proof of two hypotheses.[20] The first is that the current organizational structure does not provide sufficient space expertise or fails to apply resources properly. Secondly, only a separate service is able to provide the capability to achieve the national interests.[21] The Allard Commission report highlights the fact that the NSS organization is insufficient to ensure adequate space expertise and is unable to utilize space resources effectively.[22] In addition, the

---

[17] Harter, *Air & Space Power Journal*, Summer 2006, 67.
[18] Benjamin S. Lambeth, *Mastering the Ultimate High Ground: Next Steps in the Military Uses of Space* (Santa Monica: RAND, 2003), 63-64.
[19] Ibid., 63-64.
[20] Rife, *Air & Space Power Journal*, Spring 1999, 25.
[21] Ibid., 25.
[22] Institute for Defense Analysis, *Leadership, Management, and Organization for National Security Space: Report to Congress of the Independent Assessment Panel on the Organization and Management of National Security Space*, by A. Thomas Young, et al., Office of the Under Secretary of Defense for Policy, (Washington D.C., July 2008), ES-2.

commission concluded US national interests were in jeopardy unless the national leadership takes immediate action to unify and repair the NSS enterprise. Aerospace advocates correctly argue that all military services rely significantly on space technologies to operate and that space is an extension of their combat systems. This, however, does not justify confining space efforts within other government agencies. Again, these other agencies employ specific space professionals in order to access and exploit space. This deliberate linkage of space to aerospace, and the resulting lack of unity of effort, leads to a weakened and inefficient US space capability.[23] Surface, air, and space forces suffer when one merges their unique mediums into a singular entity.

Space is a complex environment that requires specialized knowledge and experience to leverage. A somewhat separate space force exists today, spanning numerous government agencies. The current organization, however, is ineffective and inefficient in capitalizing on the space medium. A separate space force would unify all the space professionals in a singular effort to exploit their expertise and space resources to serve the nation in this distinct medium.

Summary

Space is a unique and distinct medium from all others. Exploitation of space to achieve US national interests demands space professionals who understand this medium. Space is no more an extension of air than land is an extension of the sea. Much like its Air Force predecessor, a new space force must be separate to be most effective. Optimal exploitation of this unique medium establishes the first parallel to the creation of the Air Force and articulates the need for a US space force.

---

[23] Howard, *Rendezvous in Space*, 2010, 10.

But if we limit our efforts only to applying space technologies to existing modes of war fighting, we have undershot. . . . It is no different than all the ways our armed forces once found for airpower to support ground operations—and do no more.

Hon. Peter B. Teets
Former Undersecretary of the Air Force and
Director, National Reconnaissance Office[1]

CHAPTER 3: SPACE SYSTEMS ARE AN EVOLUTION IN TECHNOLOGY

Perhaps the most poignant American image of the evolutionary nature of space technology is that of Astronaut Neil Armstrong stepping off the lunar lander onto the moon. As he said that day, space exploration and exploitation was a "giant leap for mankind." Space systems represent an evolution in technology that provide substantial capability and are simultaneously very vulnerable. Space professionals understand these systems best and possess the requisite training and experience to manage them, their associated technology, and their proliferation. Therefore, a separate space force is required to maximize the effectiveness of this technology to better serve the nation.

Space Technology is Evolutionary

The United States' ability to put an astronaut on the moon was a singular achievement. Space technology continues to advance rapidly and provides significant advantages for the United States (US). Space technology is simultaneously evolutionary and uniquely susceptible to attack by many adversary nations around the globe. The very nature of the systems and strategies used to defeat them highlight the progression of expertise that is required in the space domain.

---

[1] Peter B. Teets, "Developing Space Power: Building on the Airpower Legacy," *Air & Space Power Journal* (Spring 2003), 14.

Space technology significantly advances the national capability. The manner in which space systems have matured, from their earliest manifestations to absolutely essential elements of national power, mirrors the rise of airpower in the last century.[2] US military forces, analogous to ground forces and airpower in the last century, have become increasingly dependent on space systems.[3] In years past, the nation might have viewed space systems as "enablers" or "mission enhancers." Today they are critical elements, and often times the singular element, that ensure effective combat operations.[4] In order to make these space systems operate successfully, a very specialized set of technological developments were necessary. These technologies, while derived from aircraft expertise, have advanced substantially.[5] Space systems can greatly enhance many missions from their vantage point. For example, space assets allow for greater intelligence gathering opportunities because sovereign overflight is not an issue. However, space systems require advanced technical design to overcome the harsh and unique environment of space. Typically, these systems cannot be repaired on orbit and are extraordinarily expensive.[6] The technology that makes these systems possible is certainly evolutionary.

While space systems clearly represent an evolution in technological prowess and the nation significantly depends on them, they are also uniquely vulnerable to attack.[7] Soon after the Union of Soviet Socialist Republics (USSR) launched the first satellite

[2] Gregory Billman, "The Inherent Limitations of Space Power: Fact or Fiction?," In *Beyond the Paths of Heaven: The Emergence of Space Power Thought* (Maxwell Air Force Base: Air University Press, September 1999), 514.

[3] Matthew Bates, "Re-fitting the Space Armada," *Airman* 54, 4 (May/June 2009), 23.

[4] Scott A. Weston, "Examining Space Warfare," *Air & Space Power Journal* 23, 1 (Spring 2009), 73.

[5] David N. Spires, *Beyond Horizons: A History of the Air Force in Space, 1947-2007* (Colorado Springs: Air Force Space Command, 2007), 136-137.

[6] Government Accountability Office, *Space Acquisitions: DOD Faces Substantial Challenges in Developing New Space Systems,* GAO-09-705T (Washington D.C., 20 May 2009), i.

[7] Weston, *Air & Space Power Journal*, Spring 2009, 73.

over the US, engineers in both nations began development of anti-satellite (ASAT) weapons. The evolutionary nature of the technology and the significant capability that space gave the space system owner drove ASAT programs. While engineers can devise ASAT systems, they are largely unable to design satellites to withstand attack. ASAT weapons have existed in one form or another for years. The US and the USSR had operational ASAT systems in the 1960s and 1970s.[8] The US system was a ground-based missile system. The Soviet version was an on-orbit satellite that could shoot a debris field at another satellite in space. In fact, the Soviet system remains on orbit to this day, presumably still capable of launching a kinetic strike against a satellite. Additionally, the US successfully tested a ground-based laser system to attack satellites in 1997 and pursued the development of multiple ASAT systems.[9] In 2008, the US demonstrated the capability to destroy a satellite on orbit by using a sea-launched missile.[10] Research in this area of technology evolution continues with new US efforts focused on co-orbital platforms to "inspect" adversary satellites.[11] Other advanced technologies can attack adversary space systems such as airborne laser and anti-ballistic missile programs.[12] Despite the relative ease with which ASAT systems can defeat satellites, the US continues to advance in the areas of space system protection and resilience.[13] Space systems are, perhaps uniquely, vulnerable to attack and degradation.

---

[8] Clayton K. S. Chun, *Defending Space: US Anti-Satellite Warfare and Space Weaponry* (New York: Osprey Publishing Limited, 2006), 32-36.

[9] Alexei Arbarov and Vladimir Dvorkin, *Outer Space: Weapons, Diplomacy, and Security* (Washington D.C.: Carnegie Endowment for International Peace, 2010), 36.

[10] Wilson W. S. Wong and James Fergusson, *Military Space Power: A Guide to the Issues* (Santa Barbara: Praeger, 2010), 93.

[11] Trevor Brown, "Soft Power and Space Weaponization," *Air & Space Power Journal* 23, 1 (Spring 2009), 66.

[12] Chun, *Defending Space*, 2006, 59.

[13] Ibid., 57.

Other nations are also testing and deploying effective ASAT technologies. China is one example of a potential adversary devoting significant resources into duplicating US space capabilities and also creating additional ASAT systems to neutralize the US space advantage.[14] The direct ascent ASAT missile program that China demonstrated in 2007 is still being refined, as are ground-based lasers and jamming systems.[15] While China pursues these programs, it publically claims that they wish only to engage in peaceful endeavors in space.[16] US satellites, however, have been "painted" or "dazzled" by Chinese lasers recently.[17] This type of action renders the satellite unable to perform its mission for a period of time. Additionally, the Chinese have developed a version of their ASAT system that defeats the anti-ballistic missile systems under development by the US.[18] Perhaps more telling, Chinese military doctrine outlines "space superiority" as a strategic goal.[19] Also significant is that China is not the only nation developing ASAT systems to counter the US space capability. Russia, for instance, joined China in calling for a space weapons ban. This stance is widely understood as a delaying tactic to give Russia time to covertly field new ASAT systems.[20] In addition to the threats from China and Russia, Iran has sufficient technology to create a brute force kinetic ASAT with their existing missiles and guidance systems.[21]

---

[14] Chun, *Defending Space*, 2006, 52.

[15] Wong and Fergusson, *Military Space Power*, 2010, 92.

[16] Phillip C. Saunders and Charles D. Lues, "China's ASAT Test: Motivations and Implications," *Joint Force Quarterly* 46 (Fall 2007), 39.

[17] Ibid., 39.

[18] Brown, *Air & Space Power Journal*, Spring 2009, 68.

[19] Roger Cliff, John Fei, et al., *Shaking the Heavens and Splitting the Earth: Chinese Air Force Employment Concepts in the 21st Century* (Santa Monica: Rand Corporation, 2011), 60.

[20] Brown, *Air & Space Power Journal*, Spring 2009, 67.

[21] Weston, *Air & Space Power Journal*, Spring 2009, 76.

Adversaries can also employ various other strategies against the evolutionary space technology. Counterspace is the more general terminology used to describe approaches designed to defeat the advantages provided by space systems. Some of these counterspace strategies are not classical ASAT techniques. For instance, jamming data links or conducting missions against ground stations (e.g. cutting power) are methods to defeat the space technology.[22] Other examples include Iraq's attempt to jam GPS signals to coalition forces and the US destruction of a ground station used by Iraq to communicate with a commercial satellite in Operation IRAQI FREEDOM.[23] Both of these actions illustrate how combatants can counter space systems in order to reduce their essential contribution to the fight. Less developed nations are able to attack space systems via computer networks, communication links, or ground stations.[24] Examples of recent successes by such nations include Libya jamming objectionable (i.e. Western) satellite signals, a Chinese dissident group hijacking a sports satellite signal in 2002 and substituting its own programming, and Iran installing satellite uplink jamming equipment in Cuba in 2006 to stop the Voice of America from reaching the Middle East.[25]

To the proponents of the aerospace view, space technology is not evolutionary, but is an extension of advanced aircraft knowledge. Some aerospace proponents argue that not all strategies to degrade space systems require specialized technologies. However, the very nature of the expertise necessary both to field and defeat space

---

[22] James G. Lee, "Counterspace Operations for Information Dominance," In *Beyond the Paths of Heaven: the Emergence of Space Power Thought* (Maxwell Air Force Base: Air University Press, 1999), 282-283.
  [23] Les Doggrell, "Operationally Responsive Space: A Vision for the Future of Military Space," *Air & Space Power Journal* 20, 2 (Summer 2006), 43.
  [24] Nader Elhefnawy, "Four Myths about Space Power," *Parameters* (2003), 126.
  [25] James B. Armor, Jr. "Viewpoint: It is Time to Create a United States Air Force Space Corps," Astropolitics 5 (2007), 276.

systems on orbit invalidates this view. Terrestrial combat systems can be effective against a space system's ground components in the same way as Army assets can defeat aircraft on the ground. Evolutionary space expertise is necessary to attack and defeat space systems in their medium of operation. Space technology continues to advance rapidly. For example, the US is also pursuing efforts to place weapons on orbit that could strike terrestrial targets with rapid and decisive results.[26] The only constant in the area of space technology is the rapid pace of change and progress.

Space technology is an evolutionary step beyond its air-based heritage. The systems provide an amazing capability but are simultaneously substantially vulnerable. Reminiscent of early years of airpower's need to be independent to exploit airpower technology, spacepower needs to be autonomous to continue to evolve.

Space Technology Requires a Separate Space Force to Maximize Effectiveness

If space systems represent an evolutionary step in technology, then space forces must also evolve to maximize space's utility. The technological challenges in the National Security Space (NSS) enterprise require a specialized and autonomous space force. Only a unified space force can effectively minimize the threat to space systems. Additionally, a distinct space force would manage the critical growth and exploitation of space knowledge. Evolutionary technology requires an evolutionary space force.

Numerous adversaries threaten US space systems with ASAT and counterspace strategies. The Allard Commission specifically noted that the US must unify NSS, unlike the current structure, to mitigate these risks. The fragmented nature of the NSS enterprise and the lack of space expertise in the acquisition process have led to billions of dollars in

---

[26] Wong and Fergusson, *Military Space Power*, 2010, 112.

additional costs and years of program delays.[27] The failures in space systems acquisition

threaten US national interests by not delivering the space capability the nation needs and

by failing to confront the threats to the space infrastructure. A unified NSS enterprise,

with a consolidated acquisition framework under a single leader, would save billions of

dollars and address system delays.[28] This inability of the current NSS structure to lead

the evolving space technology effectively has allowed other nations to close the

technology gap and threaten US space systems. To counter these growing threats against

US access to space, the National Space Policy directs government efforts to reinvigorate

space technology and "deter, defend, and defeat" adversary actions against US or allied

space assets.[29] These same themes appear in the 2012 Presidential national strategic

guidance[30] and the 2012 Joint Operational Access Concept (JOAC).[31] A separate and

unified NSS enterprise would lead this crucial effort best.

US national policies must nurture critical evolutionary space technology, which is

the foundation of the NSS enterprise, and prevent its proliferating to adversaries. The

Allard Commission pointed out that the current structure fails to achieve either objective:

"Space technology is rapidly proliferating across the globe, and many of our most

important capabilities and successes were developed and fielded with a government

---

[27] Institute for Defense Analysis, *Leadership, Management, and Organization for National Security Space: Report to Congress of the Independent Assessment Panel on the Organization and Management of National Security Space*, by A. Thomas Young, et al., Office of the Under Secretary of Defense for Policy, (Washington D.C., July 2008), 4-11.
    [28] Ibid., ES-4 - ES-5.
    [29] U.S. President, *National Space Policy* (Washington DC: Government Printing Office, June 28, 2010), 13-14.
    [30] U.S. Department of Defense, *Sustaining U.S. Global Leadership: Priorities for the 21ˢᵗ Century Defense* (Washington DC: Government Printing Office, January 2012), iii.
    [31] U.S. Department of Defense, *Joint Operational Access Concept (JOAC)* (Washington DC: Government Printing Office, 17 January 2012), 12.

technical workforce and a management structure that no longer exist."[32] According to the

US House of Representatives Select Committee on Intelligence, this stagnant or

decreasing technical capacity is due to a lack of a "comprehensive space architecture"

coupled with a failure to lead in research and development.[33] A single, unified, Space

Force would focus national priorities on developing the requisite space technology to

ensure US access and exploitation of space.[34]

In addition to technology stewardship, another current NSS shortcoming is

preventing space proliferation. Although counterintuitive, the issue is not that the NSS

enterprise allows too much technology into the marketplace, but that non-space experts

have over-limited the appropriate sale of space systems by US industry.[35] A 2008 Center

for Strategic and International Studies (CSIS) report concluded that inappropriately

applied International Traffic in Arms Regulations (ITAR) prohibited US companies from

selling non-critical space technology and spurred the growth of indigenous space

capability in adversary nations.[36] One of the explanations for this situation is the decision

to restrict technology export under ITAR rests with the US Department of State, which

may not have the technical expertise to adjudicate which technologies are critical and

which are suitable for sale. Many of the new space technology nations now sell systems

on the open market and foster the proliferation that ITAR efforts were supposed to

---

[32] Institute for Defense Analysis, *Leadership, Management, and Organization*, July 2008, i.

[33] U.S. House of Representatives, Permanent Select Committee on Intelligence, *Report on the Challenges and Recommendations for United States Overhead Architecture*, 110th Congress, 2nd Session, Report 110-914 (3 October 2008), 2.

[34] James B. Armor, Jr., "The Air Force's Other Blind Spot," *The Space Review* (15 September 2008), 7.

[35] Institute for Defense Analysis, *Leadership, Management, and Organization*, July 2008, 8-9.

[36] Center for Strategic & International Studies (CSIS), *Briefing of the Working Group on the Health of the U.S. Space Industrial Base and the Impact of Export Controls* (Washington DC: CSIS, February 2008), 8-10.

prevent.[37] A unified NSS enterprise, which aligns the efforts to protect legitimate critical

technologies and also endeavors to allow space industries to export non-critical systems,

would better serve US national interests.

Aerospace advocates contend that the existing NSS structure can confront the

threat to space assets from adversary attack, preserve and foster space technology, and

prevent proliferation. They point to US successes in exploiting space and argue that

refinements in the current architecture can lead to any necessary improvements.[38]

However, the Allard Commission concluded that it would be extremely difficult for the

current fragmented NSS enterprise to adapt efficiently or effectively to the challenges of

championing technological evolution or to counter these rising threats.[39] A unified NSS

enterprise would be able to focus the disparate elements of space expertise to protect

space systems more effectively.

Other opponents of a separate space force argue that the threats are exaggerated

and that a distinct space force would initiate an arms race that currently does not exist.[40]

They argue that the US should not deploy weapons in space. However, the 2007 ASAT

test demonstrated conclusively that China had built and deployed weapons for use in

space. From 1968-2008, the US launched 47 weapons-related payloads into orbit, 34 of

which were ASAT interceptors.[41] In other words, the nation is already engaged in an

arms race because multiple nations have already weaponized space. The US must

---

[37] National Research Council, Committee on the Rationale and Goals of the U.S. Civil Space Program, *America's Future in Space: Aligning the Civil Space Program with National Needs*, (Washington DC: National Academies Press, 2009), 51.

[38] Shawn P. Rife, "On Space-Power Separatism," *Air & Space Power Journal* 13, 1 (Spring 1999), 25.

[39] Institute for Defense Analysis, *Leadership, Management, and Organization*, July 2008, 11.

[40] Helen Caldicott and Craig Eisendrath, *War in Heaven: The Arms Race in Outer Space* (New York: The New Press, 2007), 97-98.

[41] Tamar A. Mehuron, "2009 Space Almanac," *Air Force Magazine* (August 2009), 58.

continue to put systems in place to deter, defend, and defeat enemy ASAT systems in order to confront the threat effectively.[42]   None of the various treaties regarding space (e.g. the 1967 "Outer Space Treaty") prohibits the US from placing conventional weapons in space.[43]   US research and development in ASAT technologies gives the US the ability to field ASAT systems if provided the appropriate guidance.[44]   The issue is not technological or legal, but organizational.

The current NSS structure appears unable to defend the space architecture, promote space technology, or prevent proliferation. A unified NSS enterprise is essential to confront the dual challenges of technological advocacy and threat mitigation. This distinct space force would not initiate an arms race in space – it already exists. A separate space force would provide the necessary unity to NSS.

Summary

Space systems and technology are evolutionary. The capabilities that they provide far exceed those of terrestrial systems and many of those systems significantly rely on space. Space technology is not simply a different manifestation of aerospace knowledge and it is uniquely vulnerable to poor leadership and attack. This space technology is constantly evolving and proliferating, creating new threats to US space access. Developing, nurturing, and applying this special technology by a separate space force, parallel to a new Air Force and its airpower technology, would best further US national interests.

---

[42] Everett C. Dolman and Henry F. Cooper, Jr., "Increasing the Military Uses of Space," In *Toward a Theory of Spacepower* (Washington D.C.: National Defense University Press, 2011), 102.
[43] Chun, *Defending Space*, 2006, 59.
[44] Arbarov and Dvorkin, *Outer Space*, 2010, 35.

*The customers who use space capabilities observe that there is no
responsible official who looks across all the available resources and
capabilities to seek the best solution, whether from the military,
intelligence, civilian, or commercial sector.
This represents a critical need.*
Report to Congress of the Independent Assessment Panel on the
Organization and Management of National Security Space, 2008[1]

CHAPTER 4: SPACEPOWER DEVELOPMENT REQUIRES UNIFIED AND DISTINCT LEADERSHIP, DOCTRINE, AND FUNDING

As the Allard Commission report describes above, the current leadership of the

National Security Space (NSS) enterprise is fragmented and unfocused. Without a

unified structure to lead the nation's space efforts, doctrine and funding are also

disjointed and less effective. Spacepower development requires unified and distinct

leadership, doctrine, and funding in order to serve the nation effectively.

Spacepower Development Requires Unified and Distinct Leadership

Retired Army Lieutenant General Edward Anderson, a member of the Allard

Commission, summarized the NSS leadership picture in perhaps the most succinct

manner:

> . . .the second recommendation dealt directly with leadership. What we
> found was that no one's in charge. This is not an idea we went in with,
> it's what we found. Well, when no one's in charge, everyone thinks
> they're in charge. What that creates is a situation where you get an awful
> lot of diffused direction from a multitude of sources and there is no
> focus."[2]

---

[1] Institute for Defense Analysis, *Leadership, Management, and Organization for National Security Space: Report to Congress of the Independent Assessment Panel on the Organization and Management of National Security Space*, by A. Thomas Young, et al., Office of the Under Secretary of Defense for Policy, (Washington D.C., July 2008), ES-4.
[2] Sharon L. Hartman, "An Inside Look at the Allard Commission... And That's the Way it Was," *Army Space Journal* (Summer 2009), 22.

A graphical representation of what General Anderson found appears in the introduction, Figure 2. Multiple agencies view themselves as the "lead agency" on space development. The command and control lines are fragmented and confusing, resulting in significant integration problems for a unified US space effort.[3] Indeed, both proponents and opponents of a complete reorganization of the NSS enterprise acknowledge that the space effort is an organizational "train wreck."[4] The Allard Commission noted that this failure in leadership is apparent in the routine and significant "acquisition delays, cost overruns, and performance shortfalls" in the NSS enterprise.[5] This comes as no surprise when one examines Figure 2 and attempts to ascertain where the unified leadership in NSS resides. The Allard Commission concludes that although a great many competent and professional individuals are performing at the highest levels within the system, the organization itself is "a diffuse structure that is not serving the nation well."[6]

There are many individuals within the NSS enterprise that advocate for a continuation of the current structure. Although they acknowledge there are difficulties and "seams" between separate agencies and interests, they would argue the system works well enough for a complex system. In addition, these proponents of the current system note that the diffuse nature of NSS is a design of necessity. They claim that the resident space professionals in all of the disparate organizations are necessary for mission accomplishment. However, because space training is so specialized, most organizations

---

[3] John M. Logsdon, "Emerging Domestic Structures: Organizing the Presidency for Spacepower," In *Toward a Theory of Spacepower* (Washington D.C.: National Defense University Press, 2011), 294.
[4] Richard Szafranski and Donald Kidd, "A Debate: Will the Larger Air Force Ever Accept the Space Cadre?" *Air & Space Power Journal* 20, 2 (Summer 2006), 20.
[5] Institute for Defense Analysis, *Leadership, Management, and Organization*, July 2008, ES-3.
[6] Ibid., 12.

must send their personnel to one of a select few capable agencies for training (e.g. the Air Force).[7] In fact, the US Air Force (USAF) acts as the executive agent for space matters and controls or directs a majority of the nation's space forces, platforms, and missions.[8] The proponents of the current organization argue that the success of current space assets to deliver peacetime and wartime capability is due to competent and effective leadership. Many would credit the USAF with the many successes of NSS. General James Armor concluded,

> Every major category of space system—navigation and timing, communications satellites, missile warning, weather, imagery and signals surveillance and reconnaissance, and more—owes its heritage to Air Force visionary leadership and management. . .[9]

The Allard Commission reached a different conclusion regarding the USAF's ability to be an effective steward of NSS. It summarized the USAF executive agent status as dwindling in authority since its establishment in 2001 and stating, ". . . space does not enjoy the same priority as other traditional Air Force missions."[10] Much of the explanation for the USAF's difficulties is the organizational structure of NSS.[11] The fact that NSS is able to perform as well as it does is a tribute to the space professionals and USAF leadership, not on the organizational structure. General Armor summarizes the need for organizational change in this way:

> Support of a non-existent "aerospace" regime not only prevents space from thriving, it equally undermines Air Force leadership of the vital air

---

[7] Szafranski and Kidd, *Air & Space Power Journal*, Summer 2006, 21-22.

[8] Michael L. Howard, *Rendezvous in Space – A Look in on Military Space Power* (Carlisle Barracks: U.S. Army War College, 2010), 15.

[9] James B. Armor, Jr., "The Air Force's Other Blind Spot," *The Space Review* (15 September 2008), 3.

[10] Institute for Defense Analysis, *Leadership, Management, and Organization*, July 2008, ES-4.

[11] Joan Johnson-Freese, "An Allard Commission Postmortem and the Need for a National Space Council," *Joint Forces Quarterly* 60,1 (Winter 2011), 55.

superiority mission. We've reached a point where we can no longer live with this faltering national security space mission.[12]

In short, there is a significant leadership problem within in the NSS enterprise that threatens the ability to achieve US national interests in space.

Effective leadership of the NSS enterprise requires tailored and unified leadership. Parallel to arguments made by multiple unique government entities, space forces can legitimately claim that only space professionals truly understand the distinct medium and capabilities of space.[13] Perhaps if the current system was functioning effectively, advocates of the current NSS could justify the sentiment that it "works well enough." However, the Allard Commission concluded that not only was the current NSS leadership fragmented, diffuse, confusing, and ineffective, but a "bold" reorganization is necessary.[14] One of the specific conclusions reached by the commission was that the separation of military and intelligence space has "outlived its usefulness."[15] A new leadership structure needs to unify the National Reconnaissance Office (NRO) and military space forces under one leadership architecture to prevent the "guaranteed failure" that will result in maintaining the status quo.[16] This, and other "top-to-bottom" reorganization steps, are needed to repair the leadership of the NSS enterprise.

Spacepower Requires Unified and Distinct Doctrine

General Curtis LeMay described the importance of doctrine in this way: "At the very heart of war lies doctrine. It represents the central beliefs for waging war in order to

---

[12] Armor, *The Space Review*, 15 September 2008, 7.
[13] Mark E. Harter, "Ten Propositions Regarding Space Power: The Dawn of a Space Force," *Air & Space Power Journal* 20, 2 (Summer 2006), 73.
[14] Institute for Defense Analysis, *Leadership, Management, and Organization*, July 2008, 2.
[15] Ibid., 5.
[16] Ibid., 8.

achieve victory. It is fundamental to sound judgment."[17] Spacepower is not different from ground, naval, or air forces in that respect. Effective and efficient space employment requires specialized and unified doctrine.

The military services and many civilian government agencies develop specific doctrine to describe how they contribute to national interests. This doctrine focuses the agency's efforts, clarifies its roles and missions, provides a framework for organization, and articulates its place in the whole of government approach to achieving national objectives. As the steward of the space effort, the USAF understandably contributed significantly to the current description of spacepower doctrine.[18] However, space is not simply very high altitude airspace. Spacepower cannot simply be an extension of the air medium's doctrine into space.[19] This is not appropriate or effective.[20] The characteristics of air and space are distinct enough to warrant a serious effort to create a specific spacepower doctrine.[21] Ironically, the Army similarly constricted US Army Air Forces doctrine in its early years by forcing it to conform to existing Army doctrine. The key to effective USAF doctrine was the unification and separation of its doctrine from Army influence.[22]

Parallel to airpower, spacepower needs its own distinct doctrine. As described above, multiple agencies control elements of NSS and possess their own doctrine or

---

[17] Harter, *Air & Space Power Journal*, Summer 2006, 67.
[18] Michael C. Whittington, *A Separate Space Force – An 80-Year-Old Argument* (Maxwell Air Force Base: Air University Press, May 2000), 9-10.
[19] Ibid., 9-10.
[20] Bruce M. DeBlois, "Ascendant Realms: Characteristics of Airpower and Space Power," In *The Paths of Heaven: the Evolution of Airpower Theory* (Maxwell Air Force Base: Air University Press, 1997), 563.
[21] Ibid., 563.
[22] James B. Armor, Jr. "Viewpoint: It is Time to Create a United States Air Force Space Corps," *Astropolitics* 5 (2007), 280-281.

policies. In order to bring coherence to spacepower doctrine, all of these disparate components must align into one unified and specialized doctrine. Not only would a coherent and distinct space doctrine focus space forces, it would contribute to the formation of a national strategy in space. As the National Space Strategy Project concluded, "Specifically, if a national space strategy is capabilities-based, it will remain focused on building and executing space capabilities that support national priorities, including space policy and doctrine."[23] Doctrine, therefore, is critical to the national space effort.

Aerospace advocates claim that the critical elements of airpower have parallels in the space medium. They claim that by transforming "air superiority" to "space superiority" and "counterair" to "counterspace," one can arrive at a coherent doctrine.[24] Additionally, since the doctrine is parallel, the individuals who create the doctrine and employ the systems are interchangeable. This view simply does not reflect the unique expertise required of space professionals. Space operators must possess specific skills to understand the space environment and doctrine to use spacepower effectively. As General Armor concludes, ". . . the space doctrine of the USAF has been primarily to support terrestrial operations . . . it has had the effect of neglecting the space superiority mission."[25] The need for specific space doctrine was noted by President of the United States, who outlined the importance of distinct space professionals to operational and

---

[23] National Space Strategy Project Report, *Towards a National Space Strategy* (Superior, CO: Secure World Foundation, 12 April 2010), 16.
[24] Whittington, *A Separate Space Force*, May 2000, 9-10.
[25] Armor, *The Space Review*, 15 September 2008, 4.

acquisition success in the National Space Policy.[26] Indeed, the unique talents of the US

space cadre are required to describe the doctrine essential to execute the broad range of

military space missions. This cadre must be specifically developed and nurtured to

ensure the space doctrine is correct and effective.[27] One of the key challenges the USAF

faces is the shortage of space professionals and their suboptimal career management.[28]

The space cadre requires a different set of personnel rules (e.g. allowing longer

assignment lengths in a specific duty) and procedures to develop expertise and

experience. Airpower professionals and space professionals are not interchangeable. As

a result, the doctrine that governs them and their systems are likewise distinct.

Spacepower is a unique entity, with a distinct cadre of professionals, working to

achieve US national interests. This effort requires its own unified and distinct doctrine to

serve the nation most efficiently. Like the genesis of the USAF, an evolving space force

needs the freedom to create its own doctrine.

Space Forces Require Unified and Distinct Funding

Nothing illustrates the diffuse nature of the NSS enterprise more succinctly than

the recognition that no less than eight separate requirements and funding chains exist

within the Department of Defense (DOD) to field and operate space systems.[29] When

adding the other government agencies (see Figure 2), the magnitude of the crisis in the

---

[26] U.S. President, *National Space Policy* (Washington DC: Government Printing Office, June 28, 2010), 6.
   [27] Government Accountability Office, *Report to the Chairman, Subcommittee on Strategic Forces, Committee on Armed Services, House of Representatives. Defense Space Activities: Management Actions Are Needed to Better Identify, Track, and Train Air Force Space Personnel*, GAO-06-908 (Washington D.C., Sept 2006), 1.
   [28] Institute for Defense Analysis, *Leadership, Management, and Organization*, July 2008, 4-5.
   [29] Ibid., 14.

NSS enterprise becomes clear. NSS needs a unified and distinct funding mechanism to achieve national objectives in space most efficiently.

Evaluating the funding pathways for NSS is an extremely complicated endeavor. As the primary user and provider, the DOD supports the space effort in a very convoluted manner. Utilizing the USAF as the executive agent for space, the DOD allocates almost 40% of its budget for non-Air Force specific space and intelligence functions.[30] Figure 3 depicts the 2011 USAF budget request, with estimates of how much of those funds the government diverts to NSS and related intelligence functions.[31] From the USAF budget, $30B goes to DOD classified programs, which are largely space system procurement and operations. Another $26B goes to intelligence programs, which presumably use the NSS

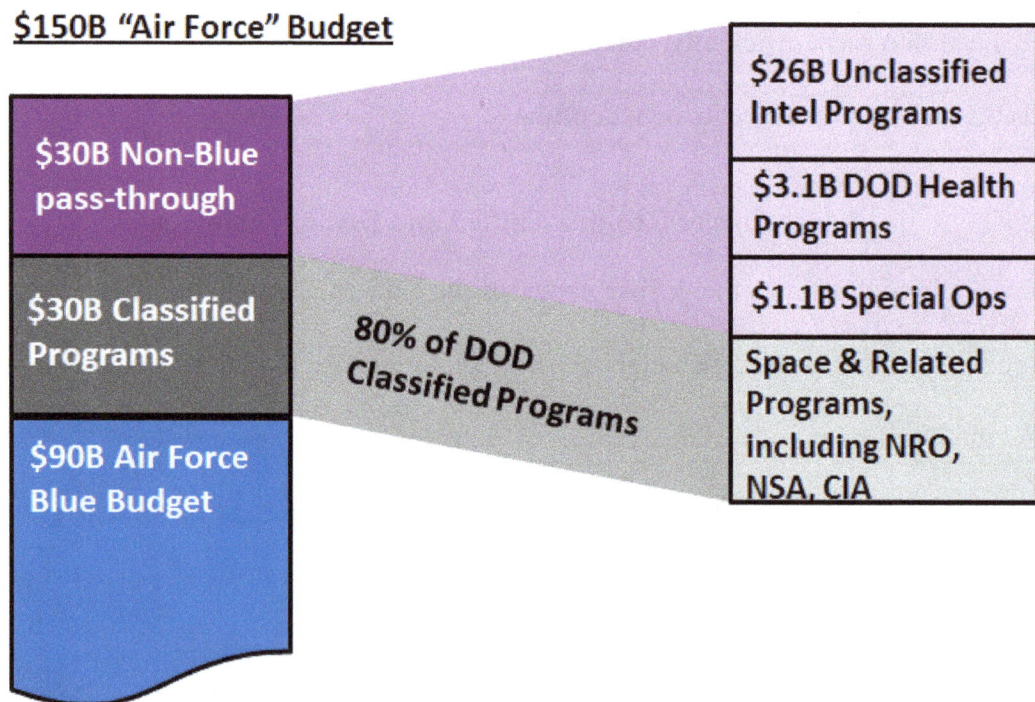

Figure 3. Space Program Funding through the Air Force Budget

_____

[30] Adam J. Hebert, "Issue Brief: Beyond the Blue Budget," *Air Force Magazine* (April 2010), 22.
[31] Ibid., 22.

systems. These funding streams "pass-through" the Air Force budget and therefore the USAF does not control them. Essentially, funding for the NSS enterprise is separate from the rest of the DOD and marginally managed by the USAF. The USAF does not possess unified space funding. Yet, the government places these funds on the Air Force ledger and they count against the total USAF portion of the DOD budget. This is especially troubling when service advocates compare the three major military services' relative share of the defense budget.[32] This places the Air Force in the untenable position of having to advocate for both the competing priorities of space systems and traditional Air Force missions.[33] The parallel to a fledgling Air Force within the US Army is striking.[34] In both cases, the parent entity attempts to balance the needs of an evolving force and the necessary and more traditional capability it possesses.

Proponents of USAF stewardship of a majority of the NSS enterprise point to decades of successes and indisputable achievements in bringing new capabilities to the warfighter. These aerospace advocates argue that the Air Force cannot easily distinguish the capabilities gained from the critical space segment causing the funding of these efforts to remain intertwined.[35] Certainly, as noted above, the Air Force bears the majority of the funding burden for NSS. Critics of Air Force stewardship note that the Air Force did not respond with vigor to space system budget cuts in 1999, but instead launched an all-out offensive to protect a likewise threatened F-22 program.[36] The pass-through nature of the space budget explains this dichotomy. With a majority of space

---

[32] Hebert, *Air Force Magazine*, April 2010, 22.
[33] Armor, *The Space Review*, 15 September 2008, 4.
[34] Armor, *Astropolitics*, 2007, 279-280.
[35] Shawn P. Rife, "On Space-Power Separatism," *Air & Space Power Journal* 13, 1 (Spring 1999), 26.
[36] Whittington, *A Separate Space Force*, May 2000, 14.

funding going to outside agencies, the USAF naturally lacks commitment to protect those

programs at the expense of necessary (traditional) airpower programs. Therefore, a tough

budget environment forces the USAF to advocate for airpower programs – because no

one else will.[37] General Horner outlined this fundamental conflict of interest in this way:

"If the Air Force clings to its ownership of space, then tradeoffs will be made between air

and space, when in fact the tradeoff should be made elsewhere."[38] Not many would

claim the USAF has been anything other than an honest and effective steward but this

funding chain must evolve for NSS to flourish.

A unified and distinct NSS funding approach is in the best interests of NSS, the

Air Force, and the nation. Currently, the USAF budget supports a bulk of NSS

procurement and operation.[39] Parallel to the Army's ownership of airpower, the

constrained budget environment is forcing the USAF to make untenable choices between

two capabilities that are essential to national interests. By making space funding distinct

from all other DOD and government budgets, the NSS enterprise could argue its own

merits without regard to Air Force funding levels. A likely outcome is that the USAF

"Blue Budget" (see Figure 3) would increase, both in real dollars and as a percentage of

the DOD defense budget, when the nation grants the large space segment separate

status.[40] This would result from rebalancing the traditional military budget between the

Army, Navy, and Air Force – without the huge space pass-through component appearing

on the USAF ledger.[41] That is, typically Congress allocates approximately a third of the

---

[37] Richard D. Moorehead, "Will We Need a Space Force?" *Military Review* (Jul/Aug 2004), 51.
[38] Rife, *Air & Space Power Journal*, Spring 1999, 21.
[39] Whittington, *A Separate Space Force*, May 2000, 13-14.
[40] Hebert, *Air Force Magazine*, April 2010, 22.
[41] Ibid., 22.

defense budget to the Army, Navy (including Marine Corps), and the Air Force. With the space budget removed for the Air Force balance sheet, a rebalance of the defense budget would lead to an increase for the Air Force budget earmarked for non-space activities. The USAF would then be able to focus on the core airpower missions so necessary for national defense.[42] Perhaps most importantly, a unified and distinct space funding system would consolidate the current diffuse system into a single organization that would be compelled to increase its efficiency, reduce duplication, and implement funding efficiencies.[43] As described in the introduction, those annual inefficiencies amount to upwards of $2 billion or almost $29 billion from FY96 to FY13.[44] In other words, the US would save a significant amount of money and further its national interests by creating a unified and distinct space funding mechanism.

Summary

The current state of the NSS enterprise parallels the early years of airpower's ascendance. Like the fledgling USAF, NSS faces significant challenges in leadership, doctrine, and funding. The current budget environment demands tough choices. These choices must not damage national interests or degrade capability. With a unified and distinct space leadership, spacepower doctrine, and NSS funding, the US can more effectively pursue its objectives.

---

[42] Robert Spalding, "America's Two Air Forces," *Air & Space Power Journal* (Summer 2009), 55.
[43] Institute for Defense Analysis, *Leadership, Management, and Organization*, July 2008, 22.
[44] Government Accountability Office, *Space Acquisitions: DOD Faces Substantial Challenges in Developing New Space Systems,* GAO-09-705T (Washington D.C., 20 May 2009), i.

The United States considers the sustainability, stability, and free access to, and use of, space vital to its national interests. . . . The United States will employ a variety of measures to help assure the use of space for all responsible parties, and, consistent with the inherent right of self-defense, deter others from interference and attack, defend our space systems and contribute to the defense of allied space systems, and, if deterrence fails, defeat efforts to attack them.

President of the United States, National Space Policy[1]

CHAPTER 5: SPACEPOWER DELIVERS STRATEGIC IMPACTS AND IS CRITICALLY IMPORTANT TO US NATIONAL INTERESTS

The President of the United States clearly summarizes the importance of the National Security Space (NSS) enterprise in the pursuit of the US national interests. Spacepower grants the nation significant capabilities and benefits. Parallel to the development of a new military department of the US Air Force (USAF), spacepower has evolved to the point where it confers strategic impacts and is critically important to the US.

Spacepower is a Strategic Resource

One way to view space is that it represents the ultimate high ground. The unique nature of the space medium and the advanced technology inherent within space systems allow them to achieve strategic advantages. The attributes of space are parallel to those of the high seas.[2] In the terrestrial oceans, free access and use of the "global commons" is in the national interests of a majority of the world's nations.[3] The "high commons" are

---

[1] U.S. President, *National Space Policy* (Washington DC: Government Printing Office, June 28, 2010), 3.
[2] John E. Shaw, "Guarding the High Ocean," *Air & Space Power Journal* 23, 1 (Spring 2009), 58.
[3] Barry R. Posen, "Command of the Commons: The Military Foundation of U.S. Hegemony," *International Security* 28,1 (Summer, 2003), 8.

likewise strategically crucial to the US and therefore the nation must vigorously defend access to space.[4] Perhaps even more than the high seas or airspace, one must uniquely consider space as the ultimate territory to operate within and to dominate.[5] Space systems can gain access to adversaries as no other terrestrial system can, with the possible exception of cyberspace. Because of this access and the importance of the capability that these space systems deliver, space is "inherently strategic."[6] Space is fundamentally strategic in that the space systems engage constantly, performing missions that yield strategic results.[7] In fact, continual access to these space assets are so essential to national interests, that the US retains the right of self-defense to ensure constant access as described in the National Space Policy[8] and the National Security Space Strategy.[9] These documents and the fundamental character of NSS systems support the conclusion that space systems deliver strategic effects and alter the strategic environment.

Proponents of the aerospace view of the NSS enterprise argue that all the strategic effects created by space systems are terrestrial and support earth-bound architectures. They point to the apparent lack of weaponization of space assets to claim that they cannot deliver strategic combat impacts. This view, however, ignores both the strategic importance of space-based intelligence and the irrefutable fact that the US and adversary

---

[4] Trevor Brown, "Soft Power and Space Weaponization," *Air & Space Power Journal* 23, 1 (Spring 2009), 69.

[5] Mark E. Harter, "Ten Propositions Regarding Space Power: The Dawn of a Space Force," *Air & Space Power Journal* 20, 2 (Summer 2006), 66.

[6] Richard Szafranski and Donald Kidd, "A Debate: Will the Larger Air Force Ever Accept the Space Cadre?" *Air & Space Power Journal* 20, 2 (Summer 2006), 19.

[7] Bruce M. DeBlois, "Ascendant Realms: Characteristics of Airpower and Space Power," In *The Paths of Heaven: the Evolution of Airpower Theory* (Maxwell Air Force Base: Air University Press, 1997), 537.

[8] U.S. President, *National Space Policy*, June 28, 2010, 3.

[9] U.S. Secretary of Defense and U.S. Director of National Intelligence, *National Security Space Strategy* (Washington DC: Government Printing Office, January 2011), 10.

nations have developed and deployed anti-satellite (ASAT) technologies. ASAT systems are capable of creating devastating strategic results. For instance, as the Chinese ASAT test demonstrated, a kinetic kill within the space medium can be the equivalent of a weapon of mass destruction.[10] A space segment attack can render large orbital regions unusable for decades and significantly decrease national capability.

The US national leadership values access to space assets highly because a space attack can have such wide reaching implications to national interests. The US could view an attack on a satellite as a form of total war instead of a simple conventional event.[11] In fact, the newly release Joint Operational Access Concept (JOAC) describes cross-domain responses to attacks in a single domain.[12] That is, the US would respond in all the domains to a strike against its space segment.[13]

The JOAC[14] and many strategic analysts predict that an adversary first strike would be against space assets because they are so strategically important.[15] This concept is diametrically opposed to the aerospace proponent that views space as an extension of the medium of air.[16] Simply because space assets create such a profound effect on terrestrial operations does not imply they do not have their own strategic impacts. Space systems, in a direct parallel to their airpower predecessors, can operate at multiple levels of warfare simultaneously. While space can provide unbeatable tactical advantages, it

---

[10] Scott A. Weston, "Examining Space Warfare," *Air & Space Power Journal* 23, 1 (Spring 2009), 80.

[11] Brown, *Air & Space Power Journal,* Spring 2009, 68.

[12] U.S. Department of Defense, *Joint Operational Access Concept (JOAC)* (Washington DC: Government Printing Office, 17 January 2012), 16.

[13] Vincent Manzo, "Deterrence and Escalation in Cross-domain Operations: Where Do Space and Cyberspace Fit?" *Strategic Forum* 272 (December 2011), 4.

[14] Ibid., 50.

[15] Manzo, *Strategic Forum*, December 2011, 1.

[16] Michael C. Whittington, *A Separate Space Force – An 80-Year-Old Argument* (Maxwell Air Force Base: Air University Press, May 2000), 7.

can concurrently provide operational level situational awareness and deliver strategic advantages like intelligence.[17] The view that space systems are limited to terrestrial support is simply short-sighted.

Despite the notion that NSS delivers strategic impacts for the nation, critics of space systems point out that these space systems are fragile and virtually undefended. The term some use is that space systems are vulnerable to a "Pearl Harbor" type attack that would significantly damage national capability. The strategic importance of these space systems prompted the Allard Commission to highlight the immediate need for a unified response by a reorganized NSS to defend against a space Pearl Harbor attack.[18] The hard truth about the national defense capability is that it is substantially dependent on an operational space segment that delivers continual strategic, operational, and tactical support.[19] In a conflict, the US would be limited more by degraded space capability than a potential enemy would be.[20] The US depends on access and use of space and its strategic benefits to support enduring national interests.

Spacepower is of Vital Importance to the Nation

Spacepower not only creates strategic impacts in support of national objectives, but the NSS enterprise is vitally important to the nation. The magnitude of space's contribution to national enduring interests mirrors that of airpower's significance at the

---

[17] Harter, *Air & Space Power Journal*, Summer 2006, 68.
[18] Institute for Defense Analysis, *Leadership, Management, and Organization for National Security Space: Report to Congress of the Independent Assessment Panel on the Organization and Management of National Security Space*, by A. Thomas Young, et al., Office of the Under Secretary of Defense for Policy, (Washington D.C., July 2008), i.
[19] Weston, *Air & Space Power Journal*, Spring 2009, 78.
[20] Ibid., 78.

Air Force's birth. As the opening quote of this chapter illustrates, the NSS enterprise has evolved into becoming one of the most critical sources of national power.

Success of the US space effort is essential to the nation's future. The Allard Commission summarizes the critical nature of NSS to national interests in this manner: "Today, US leadership in space provides a vital national advantage across the scientific, commercial, and national security realms. In particular, space is of critical importance to national intelligence and warfighting capabilities."[21] The President of the United States summarized the vital importance of space in the 2010 National Space Policy. He notes ". . . the benefits of space permeate almost every facet of our lives."[22] The President concludes that the entire world is becoming dependent on space.[23] Therefore, while space is vital to the nation, it also ". . . allow[s] people and governments around the world to see with clarity, communicate with certainty, navigate with accuracy, and operate with assurance."[24] The 2011 National Security Space Strategy echoed this analysis, and added that space "has benefited the global economy, enhanced our national security, strengthened international relationships, advanced scientific discovery, and improved our way of life."[25] The Department of Defense (DOD) and the USAF have recognized that accessing and dominating the medium of space are absolutely essential capabilities for the nation.[26] To that end, the US is pursuing all available technologies that are compliant

---

[21] Institute for Defense Analysis, *Leadership, Management, and Organization*, July 2008, ES-2.
[22] U.S. President, *National Space Policy*, June 28, 2010, 1.
[23] Ibid., 1.
[24] Ibid.
[25] U.S. Secretary of Defense, et. al, *National Security Space Strategy*, January 2011, i.
[26] Everett C. Dolman and Henry F. Cooper, Jr., "Increasing the Military Uses of Space," In *Toward a Theory of Spacepower* (Washington D.C.: National Defense University Press, 2011), 113.

with current treaties and international agreements.[27] However, other nations are engaged in ASAT and other counterspace programs to oppose US dominance in the high commons. Therefore, maintaining US national advantage in space and protecting access against adversaries are keys to retaining the vital contributions of space.

Opponents to changing the current NSS structure claim that space is an "enabling" technology and is no more important than terrestrial programs. Recent history does not support this narrow view. Space leverages all of the national centers of gravity, or sources of national power.[28] General Armor describes the vital nature of the NSS enterprise and the need for a separate space force this way:

> The United States (U.S.) has deepening dependence on space systems for economic prosperity, civil government administration, priority science and exploration programs, and national security while at the same time there is dramatic growth in competitive space capabilities and demonstrated threats to space systems globally. Despite this, the U.S. has not invested sufficient resources to meet National policy direction for capabilities to insure freedom of action in space, especially space situational awareness capabilities—the cornerstone of deterrence from space attacks. A principle reason for this shortfall is the historical absence of an organization accountable for securing the space domain like those of land, sea, and air.[29]

The integration of space into the fabric of the nation demands a comprehensive space strategy.[30] In short, space technology weaves itself into all facets of the national economy and the way one fights wars and pursues peace.

Spacepower is vitally important to the nation. Space uniquely provides capabilities that are critical to the US economy, security, and way of life. A separate

---

[27] Alexei Arbarov and Vladimir Dvorkin, *Outer Space: Weapons, Diplomacy, and Security* (Washington D.C.: Carnegie Endowment for International Peace, 2010), 80-81.
[28] Harter, *Air & Space Power Journal,* Summer 2006, 70-74.
[29] James B. Armor, Jr. "Viewpoint: It is Time to Create a United States Air Force Space Corps," *Astropolitics* 5 (2007), 273.
[30] Shaw, *Air & Space Power Journal,* Spring 2009, 57.

space force is necessary to ensure this fundamental element of national power by protecting and developing space access and exploitation. In 1947, advocates of a separate USAF made a similar call to action as airpower evolved into being vitally important to the nation. The new space capabilities and opportunities offered to the nation require recognition and engagement. Spacepower, like airpower before it, has vast potential to aid the nation in achieving its national interests.

Summary

Spacepower is a unique national capability. Space assets possess constant presence and are continually engaged in the high commons providing essential strategic contributions to national power. Vital US economic, military, and scientific efforts rely on the NSS enterprise. Like the birth of airpower in the last century, spacepower has risen in importance due to its strategic role and fundamental importance to the nation. Spacepower requires a distinct and separate service to guarantee access and utilization of this vital and strategic resource.

. . . a major top-to-bottom overhaul is needed to restore the vitality of
National Security Space, and regain and sustain the competitive
advantages afforded the United States by our space programs.
...This call to action has the highest level of urgency.
Report to Congress of the Independent Assessment Panel on the
Organization and Management of National Security Space, 2008[1]

CHAPTER 6: ESTABLISHING A US DEPARTMENT OF THE SPACE FORCE

The unique medium of space requires a separate space force to understand and

exploit it. Space technology is evolutionary and demands distinct space professionals to

maximize its effectiveness. The continual advancement of spacepower requires unified

and distinct leadership, doctrine, and funding. Spacepower has in the past, and promises

exponentially in the future, to provide strategic impacts and be vitally important to the

future of the nation. The US currently has a partially distinct space force, but it is diffuse

and inefficient. A unified and independent space force, formed from the current National

Security Space (NSS) structure, would answer the recommendations made by the Allard

Commission. The nation can construct a more efficient, effective, and responsive NSS

enterprise to ensure US space access and protect enduring national interests. The most

effective organization for NSS is a US Department of the Space Force.

Strategic Guidance

In 2008, when the Allard Commission evaluated the NSS enterprise, a clear

national strategy on space was significantly lacking.[2] A national space strategy

---

[1] Institute for Defense Analysis, *Leadership, Management, and Organization for National Security Space: Report to Congress of the Independent Assessment Panel on the Organization and Management of National Security Space,* by A. Thomas Young, et al., Office of the Under Secretary of Defense for Policy, (Washington D.C., July 2008), ES-6.
[2] Ibid., 12.

inexorably links the leadership of NSS to a clear articulation of the national space policy at the national command level.[3] Since that time, the national leadership created two documents that outline US strategy in space. This work discussed both documents, the National Space Policy[4] and the National Security Space Strategy,[5] in earlier sections. The strategic framework for the NSS enterprise exists within these documents and answers one of the challenges of the Allard Commission.

Establishing Command and Control

The most striking conclusion reached by an unbiased examination of the NSS enterprise is that the leadership of the US space effort is extraordinarily complex and largely ineffective. As previously discussed, *no one is in charge* of this element of national power that is so critical to national interests. The Allard Commission looked at a number of different alternatives to the existing NSS enterprise leadership model. One was a Space Corps, modeled after the Marine Corps and analogous to the Army Air Corps of the last century. The Space Corps would be a function of the US Air Force (USAF) but enjoy enough autonomy to clarify some of the leadership issues discovered by the Commission.[6] However, a Space Corps would not exist at the appropriate organizational level to combine military and intelligence space efforts that the Commission concludes is necessary.[7] Another alternative considered by the Commission

---

[3] National Space Strategy Project Report, *Towards a National Space Strategy* (Superior, CO: Secure World Foundation, 12 April 2010), 4.

[4] U.S. President, *National Space Policy* (Washington DC: Government Printing Office, June 28, 2010), 1.

[5] U.S. Secretary of Defense and U.S. Director of National Intelligence, *National Security Space Strategy* (Washington DC: Government Printing Office, January 2011), 1.

[6] Sharon L. Hartman, "An Inside Look at the Allard Commission… And That's the Way it Was," *Army Space Journal* (Summer 2009), 23.

[7] Hartman, *Army Space Journal*, Summer 2009, 23-24.

was to create a Department of Space that would be on the same level as the Department of Defense (DOD). This cabinet-level organization could combine a number of civilian space efforts (e.g. NASA) and all elements of military and intelligence space in one effort.[8] The Commission concluded that both the Department of Space and the Space Corps approaches violated Congressional guidance (FY 2008 DOD Appropriations Act, P.L. 110-116, Sect. 8111), which mandated that the US designate the space effort as a Major Force Program 12 under the Secretary of Defense.[9] This requires the DOD, not a specific service or a new cabinet-level department, lead the program.

With the Congressional guidance in mind, the Allard Commission proposed an organizational model for the NSS enterprise. Figure 4 illustrates this model (see list of abbreviations at the end of this work; the author inserted the dashed red outline and will describe its purpose).[10] In this architecture, the President would form a National Space Council chaired by the National Security Advisor to merge civilian space efforts. A National Security Space Authority (NSSA) would be created and serve simultaneously as both the Under Secretary of Defense for Space and the Deputy Director of National Intelligence for Space. This individual would merge military and intelligence space efforts and would provide principle oversight of a National Security Space Organization (NSSO) that combines all the functions depicted in Figure 4. Because the NSSA would serve within the DOD, this model would follow the Congressional mandate.

General Anderson, from the Allard Commission, is quick to point out the major flaw in this model. The NSSA would serve two organizations and therefore violate the

---

[8] Hartman, *Army Space Journal*, Summer 2009, 23.
[9] Ibid., 23-24.
[10] Institute for Defense Analysis, *Leadership, Management, and Organization*, July 2008, 23.

concept of unity of command.[11] General Anderson offered that the Commission

attempted to devise an organizational model to solve this issue but failed.[12] The proposal

in Figure 4 united many of the diffuse agencies and efforts in a more concise architecture

but falls short in creating a single entity in charge of NSS. The nation needs to take a

bolder step to answer the "grave"[13] challenges presented by the Allard Commission.[14]

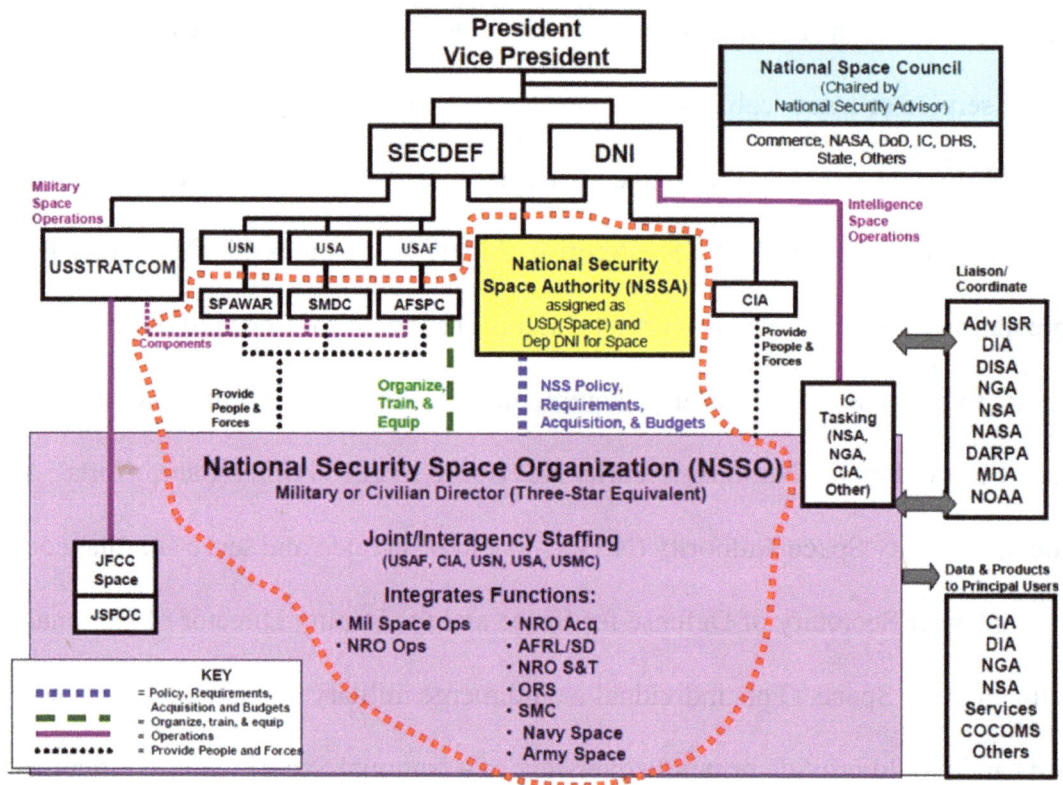

Figure 4. Allard Commission Proposed Leadership Model [10]

Using the Allard Commission proposal as a point of departure, the national

leadership can create a much more efficient and effective organization to lead the NSS

---

[11] Hartman, *Army Space Journal*, Summer 2009, 23.

[12] Ibid., 23.

[13] Institute for Defense Analysis, *Leadership, Management, and Organization*, July 2008, ES-3.

[14] Joan Johnson-Freese, "An Allard Commission Postmortem and the Need for a National Space Council," *Joint Forces Quarterly* 60,1 (Winter 2011), 56.

enterprise. In Figure 4 (see list of abbreviations), the separate military services retain the train and equip functions for space personnel. The NSSA would attempt to serve both the Secretary of Defense and the Director of National Intelligence (DNI). To correct this dual chain of command, the NSS enterprise needs a clear line of leadership from the President down to the specific space activities. Acknowledging that a bulk of the manpower and funding for NSS comes from the DOD, and more specifically the USAF (with 90% of space personnel), a new NSS architecture should originate within the DOD. The red dashed outline in Figure 4 highlights the elements of the Allard Commission proposal that must merge into a single, unified, and distinct Department of the US Space Force. The resulting architecture appears in Figure 5 (see list of abbreviations). The Space Force would be a new military department under the Secretary of Defense. This structure would comply with current Congressional guidance and clarify the lines of command and funding for the NSS enterprise. Civilian space entities (e.g. NASA) would remain apart from the merged military and intelligence space assets. The DOD would form the Space Force from existing personnel within the NSS enterprise and would therefore not require significant additional funding or infrastructure. The Space Force would possess the "train and equip" function for the space forces consolidated from all the current diffuse government agencies. Taskings for space assets would still come from DOD and DNI, and the Space Force would maintain the close relationships between space force providers and users. Unified space leadership would not degrade existing capabilities or alter support for the other military services. The Space Force would lead development of space technology and would solve the issue of proliferation with its singular expertise and focus.

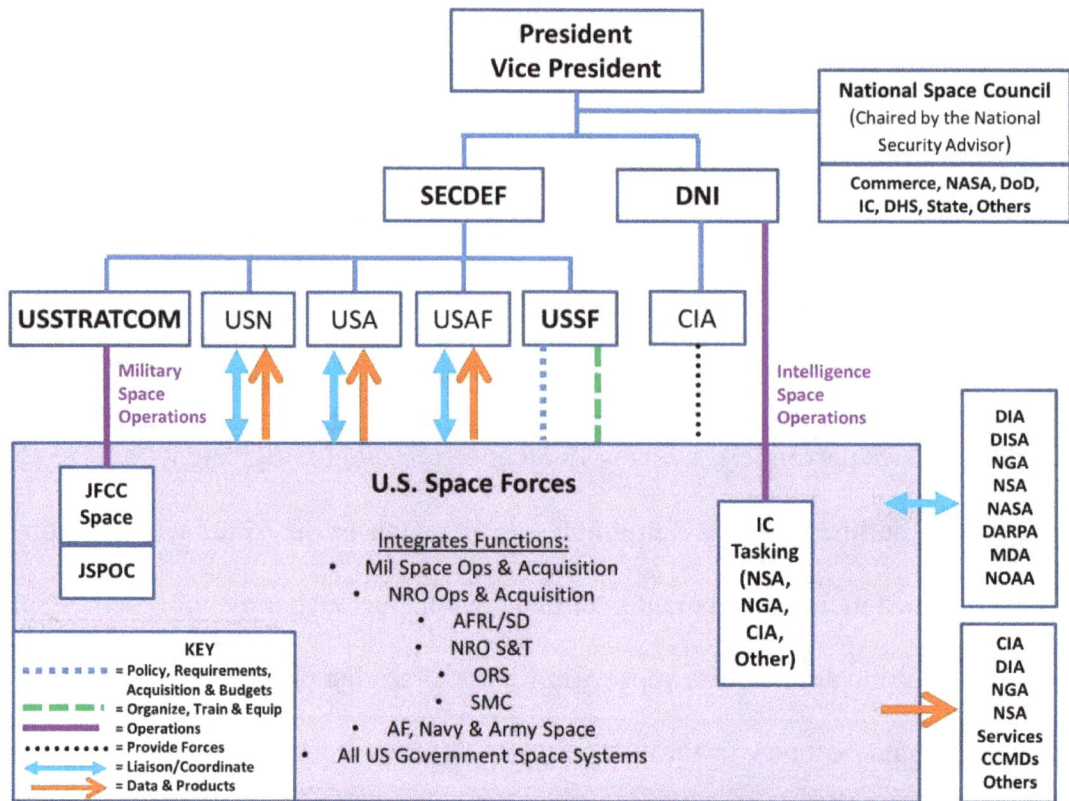

Figure 5. Proposed Department of the US Space Force

The Allard Commission proposed the interim model in Figure 4 as an incremental step to prepare the nation for an eventual independent space force.[15] Opponents of a new US Space Force argue that this evolution is unnecessary. However, as described previously in this work, a partial space force exists now. A new Department would simply consolidate the fragmented system more efficiently than the partial solution proposed by the Allard Commission. One should reserve half measures and incremental change for less important challenges or for less critical ventures. US national interests demand something more evolutionary. The current NSS structure is ineffective and immediate change is necessary. In the environment of constrained budgets and

---

[15] Institute for Defense Analysis, *Leadership, Management, and Organization*, July 2008, 21-23.

increasing threats to national interests in space, the US needs to take a bold step. A US Department of the Space Force is the optimal solution.

Establishing Acquisition Excellence and Budget Savings

One of the glaring inefficiencies in the current NSS enterprise is space systems acquisition and its resulting budgetary waste. Acquisition failures, delays, cost overruns, and the associated negative impacts on the national budget, security, and enduring interests is one of the themes in the Allard Commission. As a result of a fragmented NSS enterprise, the Commission found that "Billions of dollars have been lost and timely capability denied to US warfighters and the Intelligence Community in the past decade because of acquisition failures. The persistent space acquisition problems have been well documented by the Government Accountability Office and other independent studies."[16] The Commission concluded that a unified NSS leadership could address these issues, in particular between military and intelligence space, to save the taxpayer billions of dollars in future space acquisitions.

Opponents of reorganizing the NSS enterprise argue that this action would create a substantial cost for the government. However, General Horner argued that an independent space force would address the problems in NSS and that this new military department would be the optimal solution for the other military departments and the nation's taxpayers by improving the space enterprise and creating substantial budget savings.[17] The rationale for his conclusion is that the budget for the US Space Force would be comprised of the pass-through money in the current USAF budget (see

---

[16] Institute for Defense Analysis, *Leadership, Management, and Organization*, July 2008, 4.
[17] Steven Watkins, "Defense Trends: Is the space mission too big to handle?" *Air Force Times*, October 7, 1996, 32.

Chapter 4) which is approximately $56 billion annually. This structure could actually save a substantial amount of money from the elimination of inefficiencies and duplicated efforts estimated (see Introduction) at $2 billion annually. In fact, additional budget savings are possible from streamlined and combined space system acquisition and operation. Having the space efforts consolidated will lead to better support for all military services by eliminating the leadership problems and focusing the NSS enterprise. The US government created a separate Air Force to realize similar budget savings from the elimination of duplication and waste in airpower development.[18]

A US Space Force would reestablish acquisition excellence and realize substantial budget savings by establishing clear leadership and control of the budget process. The Allard Commission summarizes the challenge as, "Leadership for strategy, budgets, requirements, and acquisition across NSS is fragmented, resulting in an absence of clear accountability and authority . . ."[19] While the solution, proposed in Figure 4, consolidates many of the acquisition functions, it falls short of merging these efforts in the most efficient organization possible. A US Space Force (shown in Figure 5) creates a more optimal consolidation of the diffuse acquisition network. A new Department of the US Space Force would answer the Allard Commission strategic leadership challenge, reduce billions of dollars of failures, and enhance clarity, transparency, and effectiveness.

Managing a National Resource: US Space Professionals

Closely related to the topic of space acquisition excellence is that of managing the development and careers of space professionals. Space is a unique medium that

---

[18] Charles A. Stevenson, "The Story Behind the National Security Act of 1947," *Military Review* 88, 3 (May/June 2008), 20.

[19] Institute for Defense Analysis, *Leadership, Management, and Organization*, July 2008, ES-3.

possesses significant technical challenges to overcome. An effective NSS enterprise requires knowledgeable and competent individuals capable of making significant contributions to the space effort. The NSS enterprise needs to retain and cultivate these professionals to enable them to lead the Space Force.

Management of space personnel was one of the critical aspects of the NSS enterprise highlighted by the Allard Commission. Space professionals reside across multiple agencies, like NSS itself. Many of these agencies do not allow space personnel to remain attached to a particular program without damage to their career progression.[20] The result is a far less effective space force that does not gain the required proficiency and knowledge in a particular program before needing to move along an agency-normalized career path.

The Allard Commission proposed the NSSA encourage the USAF (being the agency with the bulk of the space professionals) and the Intelligence Community to modify their personnel policies to allow for longer assignments to a particular program and to protect the space force individuals from experiencing difficulties in career progression due to non-standard assignments.[21] However, the lines of command relationship in Figure 4 illustrate the fact the NSSA does not have "train and equip" authority over space forces. NSSA guidance on personnel policy is only a "recommendation" to the owning agencies. Because the command and control mechanisms outlined in Figure 4 do not address the leadership problems within NSS, this proposal cannot succeed. The USAF, for instance, cannot be compelled to modify its personnel policies by the NSSA. All the personnel for the proposed structure come from

---

[20] Institute for Defense Analysis, *Leadership, Management, and Organization*, July 2008, 24.
[21] Ibid., 24-25.

the existing agencies and they are subject to the personnel policies and career consequences of their parent agency/service.

Advocates of the present NSS structure, or of a less ambitious improvement to the NSS personnel system, argue that the current space professionals are very effective and the nation does not have enough space personnel to staff a distinct service. This author and the Allard Commission[22] both acknowledge that individual space professionals are extremely dedicated, loyal, and competent stewards of the national space system. However, the diffuse and inefficient NSS organizational structure works against these professionals and they are failing to force the system to work effectively. As an alternative to this dysfunctional architecture, the government can form the Space Force from the same pool of talented space acquisition professionals, both military and civilian, that reside within their current various agencies. This would create a synergy of talent and effort by placing all of these elements under one leadership structure, aimed at a unified objective.

A Space Force would provide the necessary architecture to solve the personnel issues in the NSS enterprise. A single service, dedicated to the space mission, would be the most appropriate vehicle to manage the space professionals and their career progression.[23] With its own paradigms of assignment length, desirable training and education, and retention programs, a Space Force would create better outcomes for space personnel. These space professionals would become the acquisition experts necessary to build future space systems and would be the cadre that generates the NSS enterprise leadership.

---

[22] Institute for Defense Analysis, *Leadership, Management, and Organization*, July 2008, 4.
[23] Ibid., ES-6.

In order to achieve national interests in space, NSS must evolve to embrace all space professionals in a single, distinct, and unified service. Space professionals are the necessary engine that drives the NSS enterprise. The space personnel architecture in NSS must evolve to maximize the efficiencies and opportunities within the space community. A US Space Force is the best vehicle to ensure the future effectiveness of space professionals.

Summary

Space is a unique and challenging environment that is vital to national interests and that requires a specialized cadre of people to access and exploit. With the current strategic guidance and Congressional mandate, the NSS enterprise must evolve to meet the challenges faced in space. A new Department of the US Space Force would clarify diffuse and ineffective leadership architecture in NSS. It would focus national efforts and reestablish acquisition excellence. In doing so, the nation would save billions of dollars at a time when budget pressures are high and continuing to dominate the national dialogue. A Space Force would also best manage the national resource of space professionals. A bold step needs to occur in the NSS enterprise. A US Space Force is the most optimal solution to the current dilemma in the NSS enterprise and holds the most promise for securing US interests in the future.

. . . significant improvements in National Security Space (NSS) leadership, management, and organization are imperative to maintain U.S. space preeminence and avert the loss of the U.S. competitive national security advantage. NSS inadequacies are unacceptable today and are likely to grow, but leadership can reverse this trend.
Report to Congress of the Independent Assessment Panel on the Organization and Management of National Security Space, 2008[1]

CONCLUSION

The time to evolve the NSS enterprise is now. The nation is facing a crisis in the space arena and these challenges threaten enduring national interests. The NSS enterprise has developed along a similar pathway as airpower's progression in the last century. The rationale for creating a US Space Force parallels the need for the genesis of the US Air Force (USAF) in the late 1940s. A US Department of the Space Force answers the challenges to the NSS enterprise and allows the US to pursue its vital interests in space more effectively.

The Immediate Need for Action

Space access and exploitation is absolutely essential to US enduring national interests. US national strategic documents iterate the importance of the NSS enterprise. Space weaves itself into the fabric of society and is necessary for the economic, military, and scientific future. Space is vital to the nation.

The current NSS enterprise is broken, with a fragmented and inefficient structure. A unified leadership of NSS is non-existent and ineffective. The acquisition process for

---

[1] Institute for Defense Analysis, *Leadership, Management, and Organization for National Security Space: Report to Congress of the Independent Assessment Panel on the Organization and Management of National Security Space*, by A. Thomas Young, et al., Office of the Under Secretary of Defense for Policy, (Washington D.C., July 2008), 1.

space systems has substantially failed over the last decade to provide the necessary oversight and direction. The US has lost billions of dollars due to inefficient practices. Entire programs have failed to arrive on time and fallen short of performance requirements. The current NSS enterprise has been unable to nurture and retain space professionals sufficiently to meet the demands of space operations and acquisitions. Simultaneous to these internal NSS obstacles are external challenges to national interests. Other nations and adversaries are developing technologies to make space a contested environment, threatening US access to and its use of space. At a time when the NSS enterprise needs to be responsive, unified, and effective, it has proven to be just the opposite.

The nation must redesign the NSS enterprise from the top down.[2] Beginning with the national strategic guidance and recognizing the vital importance of space, the US must develop the NSS architecture to confront the challenges of today and secure its place in space for the future. The nation has successfully navigated the task of creating a new organizational structure around a vital capability in the past and this example offers a framework to evaluate the future of the NSS enterprise.

Space Force Genesis Parallels the Creation of the US Air Force

The most obvious parallel to creating a new military Department of the Space Force from the NSS structure is the genesis of the USAF from the Army. The rationale used in those debates in 1947 mirror the same arguments made today about space forces and their possible future organization.

---

[2] Joan Johnson-Freese, "An Allard Commission Postmortem and the Need for a National Space Council," *Joint Forces Quarterly* 60,1 (Winter 2011), 59.

The US Army Air Forces had just finished an amazing performance in World War II and been acknowledged as the key to victory in many of the battles in the war. Most Army generals and other military professionals argued that airpower was a critical element of national power and needed to be exploited in future conflicts in order to ensure success. Spacepower possesses those same characteristics. Most military professionals would acknowledge that space is integral to current operations and a vital component in successful mission accomplishment. Space is the key to success in most of the recent US engagements.

Air is a unique medium and the third dimension of warfare. It is fundamentally different from the two surface mediums and requires a specific mindset and experience to exploit effectively. Space is also a unique medium. It is not an extension of air, but a harsh and vastly different environment compared to the terrestrial mediums. This fourth dimension of warfare requires a distinct cadre of professionals who understand it and can utilize it for national interests.

Airpower is an evolution in technology. Engineers must use technology significantly different from ground-based systems to make aircraft function within the medium of air. These technologies are highly advanced and expensive and demand a specific professional to understand and employ. Space systems are likewise technological evolutions. These space technologies are more expensive and demanding than their airpower analogues and are not extensions of aerospace approaches. A separate personnel force is required to field and operate these technologies in the unique medium of space.

The development of airpower necessitates leadership, doctrine, and funding distinct from surface forces and freedom to exploit the air environment. Liberated from competition with parochial interests within the sister services, airpower was able to develop into the critical component that it is today. Spacepower development likewise requires distinct and unified leadership, doctrine, and funding. With these key elements tied to a fragmented NSS enterprise, current space systems cannot reach their full potential to contribute to the achievement of national interests.

Airpower demonstrated conclusively that it could deliver strategic impacts and was vitally important to the nation. World War II was the prelude to a meteoric development of systems and doctrine that would ensure the nation's military dominance. Similarly, spacepower is inherently strategic and can deliver results at all levels of warfare. Additionally, space exploitation enhances the capability of the other military departments and government agencies to deliver strategic impacts. Space is vital to the nation's future.

Airpower possesses all the characteristics that demand a separate Air Force. These include a unique medium, evolutionary technology, a need for distinct leadership, doctrine, and funding that can deliver strategic results and be vitally important to the nation. Spacepower has evolved to a parallel point. Now is the time for a distinct and unified Space Force.

US Space Force: A Necessary Evolution

The US military evolved into a more efficient and effective force when the USAF was created in 1947. Airpower had reached a point where further development and contribution to national interests demanded a unified and distinct military department.

Challenges to US interests, budget constraints, and the need for efficient solutions drove the creation of the USAF. Today, the nation faces similar realities. Spacepower has evolved to the point where it must have the freedom to develop to defeat the challenges, become more efficient, and more effectively serve US national interests.

There are many that would argue that the NSS enterprise needs a smaller, more deliberate step. They claim NSS could address the space challenges with more modest changes or that creating a Space Force would be difficult or expensive. These are parochial answers that lack the courage and vision required. The NSS enterprise can evolve the most effectively with the creation of a new military Department of the Space Force. This Space Force would correct the leadership diffusion, deliver acquisition performance, save billions of taxpayer dollars, and protect and grow space expertise for the future.

The US faces significant challenges in space. In order to achieve US national interests within a very constrained fiscal environment, a new US Department of the Space Force is a necessary evolution. Like airpower before it, spacepower has reached a crossroads. Space is as necessary for national success as airpower was in 1947. Now is the time to create a Space Force and secure the nation's future in the high frontier.

LIST OF ABBREVIATIONS

Acq – Acquisitions
Adv ISR – Advanced Intelligence, Surveillance, and Reconnaissance
AF – Air Force
AFMC – Air Force Material Command
AFRL – Air Force Research Laboratory
AFSPC – Air Force Space Command
AIAA – American Institute of Aeronautics and Astronautics
ARSTRAT – Army Forces Strategic Command
ASAT – Anti-Satellite
ASD(NII) – Assistant Secretary of Defense for Networks & Information Integration
CCMDs – Combatant Commands
CIA – Central Intelligence Agency
CJCS – Chairman of the Joint Chiefs of Staff
CSIS – Center for Strategic and International Studies
CTF – Combined Task Force
DARPA – Defense Advanced Research Projects Agency
Dep DNI – Deputy Director of National Intelligence
DHS – Department of Homeland Security
DIA – Defense Intelligence Agency
Dir – Director
DISA – Defense Information Systems Agency
DNI – Director of National Intelligence
DOD – Department of Defense
EA – Executive Agent
FY – Fiscal Year
GSI – Global Strike and Integration
GNO – Global Network Operations
IC – Intelligence Community
IMD – Integrated Missile Defense
ISR – Intelligence, Surveillance, and Reconnaissance
ITAR – International Traffic in Arms Regulations
JFCC – Joint Functional Component Command
JOAC – Joint Operational Access Concept
JSpOC – Joint Space Operations Center
JTF – Joint Task Force
MDA – Missile Defense Agency
MUOS SPO (Navy) – Mobile User Objective System, System Program Office (Navy)
NASA – National Aeronautics and Space Administration
NGA – National Geospatial-Intelligence Agency
NOAA – National Oceanic and Atmospheric Administration
NRO – National Reconnaissance Office
NROC – National Reconnaissance Operations Center
NSA – National Security Agency

NSC – National Security Council
NSS – National Security Space
NSSA – National Security Space Authority
NSSO – National Security Space Organization
NW – Network Warfare
OMB – Office of Management and Budget
ORS – Operationally Responsive Space Office (DOD)
OSTP – Office of Science and Technology Policy
PEO – US Navy Program Executive Office for Space Systems
S&T – Science and Technology
SecAF – Secretary of the Air Force
SecArmy – Secretary of the Army
SECDEF – Secretary of Defense
SecNavy – Secretary of the Navy
SMC – Space and Missile Center
SMDC – Space and Missile Defense Command (US Army)
SPAWAR – Space and Naval Warfare Systems Command
STRATCOM – United States Strategic Command
US – United States
USA – United States Army
USAF – United States Air Force
USAAF – United States Army Air Forces
USD(AT&L) – Under Secretary of Defense for Acquisition, Technology and Logistics
USD(I) – Under Secretary of Defense for Intelligence
USD(P) – Under Secretary of Defense for Policy
USD(Space) – Under Secretary of Defense for Space
USSF – United States Space Force
USN – United States Navy
USSR – Union of Soviet Socialist Republics
USSTRATCOM – United States Strategic Command
WWI – World War I
WWII – World War II

BIBLIOGRAPHY

Arbarov, Alexei, and Vladimir Dvorkin. *Outer Space: Weapons, Diplomacy, and Security.* Washington D.C.: Carnegie Endowment for International Peace, 2010.

Armor, James B. Jr. "The Air Force's Other Blind Spot." *The Space Review* (15 September 2008): 1-8.

————. "Viewpoint: It is Time to Create a United States Air Force Space Corps." *Astropolitics* 5 (2007): 273-288.

Bates, Matthew. "Re-fitting the Space Armada." *Airman* 54, 4 (May/June 2009): 20-23.

Billman, Gregory. "The Inherent Limitations of Space Power: Fact or Fiction?" In *Beyond the Paths of Heaven: The Emergence of Space Power Thought,* 507-568. Maxwell Air Force Base: Air University Press, September 1999.

Brown, Trevor. "Soft Power and Space Weaponization." *Air & Space Power Journal* 23, 1 (Spring 2009): 66-72.

Brunner, William W. III. "National Security Implications of Inexpensive Space Access," In *Beyond the Paths of Heaven: the Emergence of Space Power Thought,* 365-435. Maxwell Air Force Base: Air University Press, September 1999.

Butler, Amy. "Adrift in Space." *Aviation Week & Space Technology.* 169, 14 (13 October 2008): 34.

Caldicott, Helen, and Craig Eisendrath. *War in Heaven: The Arms Race in Outer Space.* New York: The New Press, 2007.

Center for Strategic & International Studies. *Briefing of the Working Group on the Health of the U.S. Space Industrial Base and the Impact of Export Controls.* Washington DC: CSIS, February 2008.

Chairman of the Joint Chiefs of Staff. *The National Military Strategy of the United States of America.* Washington DC: Government Printing Office, 2011.

Chun, Clayton K. S. *Defending Space: US Anti-Satellite Warfare and Space Weaponry.* New York: Osprey Publishing Limited, 2006.

Cliff, Roger, and John Fei, et al. *Shaking the Heavens and Splitting the Earth: Chinese Air Force Employment Concepts in the 21st Century.* Santa Monica: Rand Corporation, 2011.

Clodfelter, Mark A. "Molding Airpower Convictions: Development and Legacy of William Mitchell's Strategic Thought," In *The Paths of Heaven: the Evolution of Airpower Theory*, 79-114. Maxwell Air Force Base: Air University Press, 1997.

Committee on U.S. Space Leadership. "Memorandum for the President: America's Leadership in Space." *Space Policy* (10 March 2009): 1-9.

DeBlois, Bruce M. "Ascendant Realms: Characteristics of Airpower and Space Power," In *The Paths of Heaven: the Evolution of Airpower Theory,* 529-578. Maxwell Air Force Base: Air University Press, 1997.

Doggrell, Les. "Operationally Responsive Space: A Vision for the Future of Military Space." *Air & Space Power Journal* 20, 2 (Summer 2006): 42-49.

Dolman, Everett C. and Cooper, Henry F. Jr. "Increasing the Military Uses of Space," In *Toward a Theory of Spacepower*, 97-117, Washington D.C.: National Defense University Press, 2011.

Elder, Robert J. "Air-Mindedness." *Air & Space Power Journal* 23, 3 (Fall 2009): 11-18.

Elhefnawy, Nader. "Four Myths about Space Power." *Parameters* (2003): 124-132.

Farley, Robert. "Abolish the Air Force." *The American Prospect* 18, 11 (Nov 2007): 34-37.

Fogleman, Ronald R. "Aerospace Doctrine: More Than Just a Theory." *Airpower Journal* (Summer 1996): 40-47.

Gentile, Gian P. "A-bombs, budgets, and morality: Using the Strategic Bombing Survey." *Air Power History* 44, 1 (Spring 1997): 18-31.

Glines, C. V. "The Long Road to an Independent Air Force." *Aviation Story* 18, 1 (Sep 2007): 30-41.

Government Accountability Office. *Report to the Chairman, Subcommittee on Strategic Forces, Committee on Armed Services, House of Representatives. Defense Space Activities: Management Actions Are Needed to Better Identify, Track, and Train Air Force Space Personnel.* GAO-06-908. Washington D.C., Sept 2006.

———. *Space Acquisitions: DOD Faces Substantial Challenges in Developing New Space Systems.* GAO-09-705T. Washington D.C., 20 May 2009.

———. *Space Acquisitions: Major Space Programs Still at Risk for Cost and Schedule Increases.* GAO-08-552T. Washington D.C., 4 May 2008.

Harter, Mark E. "Ten Propositions Regarding Space Power: The Dawn of a Space Force." *Air & Space Power Journal* 20, 2 (Summer 2006): 64-126.

Hartman, Sharon L. "An Inside Look at the Allard Commission… And That's the Way it Was." *Army Space Journal* (Summer 2009): 18-27.

Hebert, Adam J. "Issue Brief: Beyond the Blue Budget." *Air Force Magazine* (April 2010): 22.

Howard, Michael L. *Rendezvous in Space – A Look in on Military Space Power.* Carlisle Barracks: U.S. Army War College, 2010.

Institute for Defense Analysis. *Leadership, Management, and Organization for National Security Space: Report to Congress of the Independent Assessment Panel on the Organization and Management of National Security Space*, by A. Thomas Young, et al. Office of the Under Secretary of Defense for Policy. Washington D.C., July 2008.

Johnson-Freese, Joan. "An Allard Commission Postmortem and the Need for a National Space Council." *Joint Forces Quarterly* 60, 1 (Winter 2011): 54-60.

Lambeth, Benjamin S. *Mastering the Ultimate High Ground: Next Steps in the Military Uses of Space.* Santa Monica: RAND, 2003.

Lee, James G. "Counterspace Operations for Information Dominance," In *Beyond the Paths of Heaven: the Emergence of Space Power Thought*, 249-301. Maxwell Air Force Base: Air University Press, 1999.

Liddell-Hart, B. H., ed. *The Rommel Papers.* New York: Da Capo Press, 1953.

Logsdon, John M. "Emerging Domestic Structures: Organizing the Presidency for Spacepower," In *Toward a Theory of Spacepower*, 277-297, Washington D.C.: National Defense University Press, 2011.

Manzo, Vincent. "Deterrence and Escalation in Cross-domain Operations: Where Do Space and Cyberspace Fit?" *Strategic Forum* 272 (December 2011): 1-8.

Mehuron, Tamar A. "2009 Space Almanac." *Air Force Magazine* (August 2009): 52-65.

Millsap, Ralph, and Posey, D. B. "Organizational Options for the Future Aerospace Force." *Aerospace Power Journal* 14, 2 (Summer 2000): 48-56.

Monahan, George H. *The Army-Navy Contest for Control of Land-Based Antisubmarine Aviation and the Military Unification Debate, 1942-1948.* Ann Arbor: Proquest, May 2011.

Moorehead, Richard D. "Will We Need a Space Force?" *Military Review* (Jul/Aug 2004): 50-53.

National Research Council. Committee on the Rationale and Goals of the U.S. Civil Space Program. *America's Future in Space: Aligning the Civil Space Program with National Needs*. Washington DC: National Academies Press, 2009.

National Space Strategy Project Report. *Towards a National Space Strategy*. Superior, CO: Secure World Foundation, 12 April 2010.

Posen, Barry R. "Command of the Commons: The Military Foundation of U.S. Hegemony." *International Security* 28, 1 (Summer, 2003): 5-46.

Rife, Shawn P. "On Space-Power Separatism." *Air & Space Power Journal* 13, 1 (Spring 1999): 21-31.

Saunders, Phillip C., and Charles D. Lues. "China's ASAT Test: Motivations and Implications." *Joint Force Quarterly* 46 (Fall 2007): 39-45.

Shaud, John A., and Adam B. Lowther. "An Air Force Strategic Vision for 2020-2030." *Strategic Studies Quarterly* (Spring 2011): 8-31.

Shaw, John E. "Guarding the High Ocean." *Air & Space Power Journal* 23, 1 (Spring 2009): 55-65.

Spalding, Robert. "America's Two Air Forces." *Air & Space Power Journal* (Summer 2009): 51-56.

Spires, David N. *Beyond Horizons: A History of the Air Force in Space, 1947-2007*. Colorado Springs: Air Force Space Command, 2007.

Stevenson, Charles A. "The Story Behind the National Security Act of 1947." *Military Review* 88, 3 (May/June 2008): 13-20.

Szafranski, Richard, and Donald Kidd. "A Debate: Will the Larger Air Force Ever Accept the Space Cadre?" *Air & Space Power Journal* 20, 2 (Summer 2006): 19-25.

Teets, Peter B. "Developing Space Power: Building on the Airpower Legacy." *Air & Space Power Journal* (Spring 2003): 11-15.

U.S. Department of Defense. *Defense Budget Priorities and Choices*. Washington DC: Government Printing Office, January 2012.

————. *Joint Operational Access Concept (JOAC)*. Washington DC: Government Printing Office, 27 January 2012.

———. *Quadrennial Defense Review Report.* Washington DC: Government Printing Office, February 2010.

———. *Sustaining U.S. Global Leadership: Priorities for the 21st Century Defense.* Washington DC: Government Printing Office, January 2012.

U.S. House of Representatives, Permanent Select Committee on Intelligence, *Report on the Challenges and Recommendations for United States Overhead Architecture*, 110th Congress, 2nd Session, Report 110-914, 3 October 2008.

U.S. President. *National Security Strategy.* Washington DC: Government Printing Office, May 2010.

———. *National Space Policy.* Washington DC: Government Printing Office, June 28, 2010.

U.S. Secretary of Defense and U.S. Director of National Intelligence. *National Security Space Strategy.* Washington DC: Government Printing Office, January 2011.

Watkins, Steven. "Defense Trends: Is the space mission too big to handle?" *Air Force Times* (October 7, 1996): 32-33.

Westenhoff, Charles M. "Why we Need an Air Force." *Joint Force Quarterly* (Autumn/Winter 1994-95): 62-67.

Weston, Scott A. "Examining Space Warfare." *Air & Space Power Journal* 23, 1 (Spring 2009): 73-127.

Wolk, Herman S. "Ike and the Air Force." *Air Force Magazine* (April 2006): 84-88.

———. *Toward Independence: The Emergence of the U.S. Air Force 1945-1947.* Bolling Air Force Base: Air Force History and Museums Program, 1996.

Wong, Wilson W. S., and James Fergusson. *Military Space Power: A Guide to the Issues.* Santa Barbara: Praeger, 2010.

Whittington, Michael C. *A Separate Space Force – An 80-Year-Old Argument.* Maxwell Air Force Base: Air University Press, May 2000.

Dr. John D. "Toast" Cinnamon, Ph.D. authored this work in 2012 while he was an active-duty Air Force Officer. The initial reaction to this analysis was one of resistance. In 2019, this document was foundational to the efforts to create a separate US Space Force. Colonel Cinnamon retired in 2018 as the Permanent Professor & Head of the Department of Aeronautics at the US Air Force Academy after 27+ years of service. Toast has a Bachelor of Science in Engineering Sciences (Space Systems Design) from the USAF Academy, a Master of Science in Aerospace Engineering (Space Systems Design) from the University of Texas at Austin, and a Ph.D. in Aeronautical Engineering from the Air Force Institute of Technology, as well as a Master of Science in Campaign Planning & Strategy from the National Defense University. John was a Command Pilot in the US Air Force and flew more than 4500 hours in various aircraft in operations around the globe. John now serves as a Senior Technical Leader for the US Space Force.